M000111311

Math Skills Mind Benders

BY
CINDY BARDEN AND JOSEPH A. KUNICKI, Ph.D.

COPYRIGHT © 2010 Mark Twain Media, Inc.

ISBN 978-1-58037-557-3

Printing No. CD-404132

Mark Twain Media, Inc., Publishers
Distributed by Carson-Dellosa Publishing LLC

Visit us at www.carsondellosa.com

HPS 221293

Table of Contents

Introduction

Math Skills Mind Benders is designed to supplement your math curriculum by providing challenging and fun activities related to vital mathematical skills appropriate for grades five through eight and beyond. Activities from a range of skills are provided to give teachers differentiated instruction materials for students of varying skill levels. Concepts and skills covered are listed at the top left of each page. A graduated bar at the top right indicates the suggested grade level of each activity.

This book uses brain teasers, puzzles, games, pictures, stories, and other fun activities to reinforce skills appropriate for fifth- through eighth-grade mathematics curriculum at home or in the classroom using National Council of Teachers of Mathematics (NCTM) guidelines to promote essential mathematical skills.

- **Number and Operations** – Students deepen their understanding of basic operations, number sense, place value, fractions, decimals, percents, and integers, and they become proficient in using them to solve problems.

- **Algebra** – Activities are used as a method of understanding variables, expressions, equations, patterns, functions, and generalizations.

- **Geometry** – Students investigate relationships by drawing, measuring, visualizing, comparing, transforming, and classifying geometric objects.

- **Measurement** – Students build on their formal and informal experiences with measurable attributes like length, area, and volume; with units of measurement; and with systems of measurement.

- **Data Analysis and Probability** – Exercises emphasize techniques to collect, describe, organize, analyze, evaluate, and interpret data.

- **Problem Solving** – Opportunities for inductive and deductive reasoning are provided through logic-based activities.

- **Reasoning and Proof** – Students deepen the evaluations of their assertions and conjectures and use inductive and deductive reasoning to formulate mathematical arguments.

- **Communications** – Verbal and written skills are learned through math games and stories.

- **Connections** – Students learn to associate math skills with other subjects as well as the world outside the classroom through activities related to everyday math situations, history, and social studies.

- **Representations** – Students learn to recognize, compare, and use an array of representational forms for fractions, decimals, percents, integers, and they also learn to use representational forms, such as exponential and scientific notation.

Name: _____ Date: _____

Skip count/Multiplication warm-up

Level: 4 5 6 7 8

Simply A-Mazing

Directions: Read the rhymes, then draw lines to show the path Gordie needs to follow to reach his goal. Gordie can move one square at a time, up, down, across, or diagonally.

A. Start with three, add three, and then, keep counting by three to the very end.

START

7	9	12	6	12
3	6	24	15	57	54
16	27	21	18	51	60
33	30	42	45	48	63
36	39	72	69	66	43
27	75	78	81	84	END

B. Four plus four, and then four more. Keep counting by four 'til you reach the door.

9	46	18	16	4	START
16	21	20	12	8	10
4	24	25	36	40	30
54	28	32	64	44	48
76	72	68	60	56	52
84	80	74	8	42	24

Today's Riddle: Why was the gorilla surprised when corn grew out of his ears?

Name: _____   Date: _____

Sequence decimals

Level: | 4 | 5 | 6 | 7 | 8 |

Riddle Me

Directions: Number the decimals in order from lowest to highest on the blanks below the chart. Then, to answer the riddle, write the letters that match the numbers in order.

0.3	0.1	0.7	0.5	0.9	0.6	0.4	0.8	0.2	0.53	0.76	0.41	0.99
h	i	b	p	m	o	a	e	t	r	l	d	s

___ __1__ ___ ___ ___ ___ ___ ___ ___ ___ ___ ___ ___

Riddle #1: Why did the math book go to the doctor?

$\frac{I}{1}$ $\frac{}{2}$ $\frac{}{3}$ $\frac{}{4}$ $\frac{}{5}$

$\frac{}{6}$ $\frac{}{7}$ $\frac{}{8}$ $\frac{}{9}$ $\frac{}{10}$ $\frac{}{11}$ $\frac{}{12}$ $\frac{}{13}$!

• •

0.93	0.33	0.79	0.42	0.11	0.97	0.64	0.58	0.16	0.81	0.24	0.45	0.271	0.59
e	o	h	u	f	e	t	o	i	r	v	t	e	f

___ ___ ___ ___ ___ ___ ___ ___ ___ ___ ___ ___ ___ ___

Riddle #2: Do you know how many people have trouble with fractions?

$\frac{}{1}$ $\frac{}{2}$ $\frac{}{3}$ $\frac{}{4}$ $\frac{}{5}$ $\frac{}{6}$ $\frac{}{7}$

$\frac{}{8}$ $\frac{}{9}$ $\frac{}{10}$ $\frac{}{11}$ $\frac{}{12}$ $\frac{}{13}$ $\frac{}{14}$

Name: _____ Date: _____

Find prime numbers

Level: 4 5 6 7 8

Prime Time

Directions: Follow the steps below to find all the prime numbers from 1 to 100.

A. Cross out all numbers that can be divided evenly by 2, except 2. Circle the 1 and the 2.

   1 is a prime number because it can only be divided by itself.

   2 is a prime number because it can only be divided evenly by itself and 1.

B. Cross out all numbers that can be divided evenly by 3, except 3. Circle the 3.

C. Is 3 a prime number? _____ Why or why not? _____

_____

D. Is 4 a prime number? _____ Why or why not? _____

_____

E. Since 4 has already been crossed out, go on to 5. Cross out all numbers that can be divided evenly by 5, except 5. Circle the 5.

F. Continue until all prime numbers are circled.

1	2	3	4	5	6	7	8	9	10
11	12	13	14	15	16	17	18	19	20
21	22	23	24	25	26	27	28	29	30
31	32	33	34	35	36	37	38	39	40
41	42	43	44	45	46	47	48	49	50
51	52	53	54	55	56	57	58	59	60
61	62	63	64	65	66	67	68	69	70
71	72	73	74	75	76	77	78	79	80
81	82	83	84	85	86	87	88	89	90
91	92	93	94	95	96	97	98	99	100

4

Name: _____   Date: _____

Compare and order integers   **Level:** 4   5   6   7   8

On a January day, these temperatures were reported.

A.   Number the cities from 1 (coldest) to 5 (warmest).

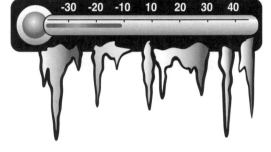

    -11°F   Boston   _____

    - 6°F   Chicago   _____

    -14°F   Detroit   _____

    -21°F   Minneapolis   _____

     3°F   Pittsburgh   _____

Compare. Write < (less than) or > (greater than) in the blanks.

B.   -4° ____ -2°   C.   -11° ____ -12°   D.   -6° ____ -12°

E.   -3° ____ 0°   F.   7° ____ -1°   G.   -5° ____ -7°

Write the integers in order from the coldest to the warmest.

H.   4   -7   2   -6   0   3

    _____

I.   1   4   -9   6   -8   -12   0

    _____

J.   5   -6   7   -8   4   -3   2

    _____

Write the next three integers in the pattern.

K.   5   3   1   -1   ____ ____ ____   L.   -7   -5   -3   -1   ____ ____ ____

M.   10   5   0   -5   ____ ____ ____   N.   -20   -15   -10   -5   ____ ____ ____

Describe the weather on the coldest day you've ever experienced. How cold was it?

_____

_____

_____

_____

Name: _____   Date: _____

Place value/Compare large numbers   **Level:** | 4 | 5 | 6 | 7 | 8 |

Commas Help

Commas help us read large numbers.

Use a comma to separate hundreds from thousands.

Examples: 34,567 $218,500

Use a comma to separate thousands from millions.

Examples: 5,426,689 $215,561,073

Directions: Add commas where needed.

A. $5 3 5 6 3   B.   2 8 4 1 6 4   C.   1 3 6 9 0 0 1

D. $2 0 4 6 0 1 5 9   E.   4 3 2 6 8 9 0   F.   9 0 1 2 6 7 8 9 1

Directions: Add commas where needed. Circle the larger number in each set.

G. $5 3 4 7 $5 3 4 4 7   H.   5 1 4 2 2 2   5 1 4 2 2

I.   1 6 5 7 8 0 1   1 6 5 7 8 0 1 1   J. $4 3 7 8 9 . 0 8 $4 3 7 9 9 . 0 8

K. 9 2 3 5 9 9 4   9 2 3 5 9 9 9 4   L.   2 3 1 0 7 8 4 6 7   2 3 1 0 7 8 6 4

Directions: Write the numbers. Don't forget the commas.

M.   Thirty-five million, six hundred thousand _____

N.   Five thousand, two hundred sixteen dollars _____

O.   Eighty-seven million, nine hundred seven _____

Name: _____   Date: _____

Place Value   Level: ▮ 4   5   6   7   8

Place Value Puzzle

Directions: In the puzzle grid below, write the number represented by each clue.

ACROSS

A. Three thousand, sixty-nine
D. 2 hundreds, 7 tens
F. one ten
G. 9 x 9
H. forty-two thousand, seven
K. 4 tens and 6 ones
M. 90 thousands, 7 hundreds, 3 ones
N. 37 x 2
O. 100 - 47
P. 60 thousands, 3 hundreds, 3 ones
R. thirty-five
S. 92 thousands, 4 hundreds, 1 ten
T. sixty-eight
V. eighty-two
W. 2 hundreds, 3 tens, 2 ones
X. nine thousand nine

DOWN

A. three hundred four thousand, nine hundred fifty-three
B. 6 thousands, 1 hundred, 7 ones
C. nine hundred thousand, sixty-nine
D. 7 x 4
E. seven hundred fourteen thousand, seven hundred one
I. 203 thousands, 5 hundreds, 6 tens, 3 ones
J. seven hundred thirty thousand, two hundred eighty-nine
L. six hundred forty-three thousand, nineteen
Q. 3 thousands, 4 hundreds, 2 tens
U. eighty-two

Name: _____   Date: _____

Add three-digit numbers/Identify place value

Level: | 4 | 5 | 6 | 7 | 8 |

Place Value Race

Directions: Use several decks of cards, ace through 9 (ace = 1). Each player will need a pencil, scrap paper, and a Place Value Race Card. (see below)

1. Shuffle cards and place them face down.

2. Draw six cards and lay them face up like this:

3. Write an addition equation using those numbers.

4. Write the answer to the equation.

5. Find the corresponding place values of the numbers in the answer on the Place Value Race Card and X them out. Cross out only numbers that haven't been used before.

6. Take turns until one player crosses out all numbers on his or her Place Value Race Card.

   Example: Player draws these cards: 2 4 3 8 5 9
   Write and solve the equation:

$$\begin{array}{r} 243 \\ + 859 \\ \hline 1102 \end{array}$$

   Cross off 1 in thousands row, 1 in hundreds row, 0 in tens row, and 2 in ones row.

- ✂

Ones	0	1	2	3	4	5	6	7	8	9	
Tens	0	1	2	3	4	5	6	7	8	9	**Place Value Race Card**
Hundreds	0	1	2	3	4	5	6	7	8	9	
Thousands	0	1	2	3	4	5	6	7	8	9	

- ✂

Ones	0	1	2	3	4	5	6	7	8	9	
Tens	0	1	2	3	4	5	6	7	8	9	**Place Value Race Card**
Hundreds	0	1	2	3	4	5	6	7	8	9	
Thousands	0	1	2	3	4	5	6	7	8	9	

Name: _____   Date: _____

Round to nearest hundred

Level: | 4 | 5 | 6 | 7 | 8 |

Round-Up

1. You will need a deck of cards from ace through 9. Each player needs a colored pencil and a Round-Up game card. (ace = 1)

2. Players take turns drawing three cards and placing them like this:

3. Round the resulting three-digit number to the nearest hundred. If the answer is correct, the player colors the longhorn with the matching number on his or her Round-Up game card.

4. If no longhorn remains on a player's Round-Up game card to match the answer, the player skips a turn. The first player with all longhorns colored completes the round-up and wins the game.

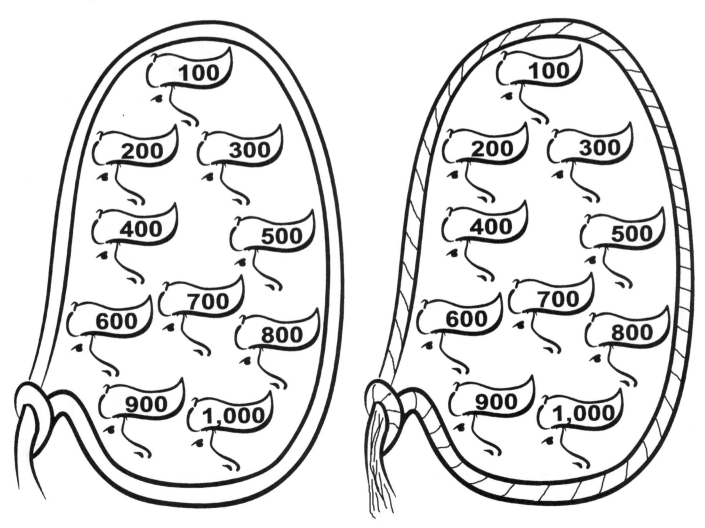

Name: _____   Date: _____

Place value   **Level:** ▓▓▓▓ 5 6 7 8

Get the Point?

Rewrite each number on the chart.

A.   4,356,087.01   B.   Two million and seven

C.   400,972.1469   D.   457 thousandths

E.   3,271.570154   F.   Twenty-six and 57 hundredths

G.   0.592186   H.   3 millionths

I.   234,567.12345   J.   Seven million and one tenth

K.   1,007,100.007007   L.   6,256.187356

	Millions	Hundred Thousands	Ten Thousands	Thousands	Hundreds	Tens	Ones		Tenths	Hundredths	Thousandths	Ten-thousandths	Hundred thousandths	Millionths
A.								.						
B.								.						
C.								.						
D.								.						
E.								.						
F.								.						
G.								.						
H.								.						
I.								.						
J.								.						
K.								.						
L.								.						

Did You Know? One pencil can draw a line about $33\frac{1}{2}$ miles long.

Name: _____   Date: _____

Identify process/Write equations

Level: | 4 | 5 | 6 | 7 | 8 |

What Should You Do?

Directions: Circle A (add), S (subtract), M (multiply) or D (divide) to show the process needed to find the answer to each story. Then write the equation.

1. A new library has 1,307,985 books to unpack and put on shelves. Each shelf holds 57 books. How many shelves are needed?

   A   S   M   D   Equation: _____

2. Vivian's Video rented 45 movies on Monday, 28 on Tuesday, 59 on Wednesday, 74 on Thursday, 126 on Friday, 184 on Saturday, and 201 on Sunday. How many movies did they rent that week?

   A   S   M   D   Equation: _____

3. A squirrel buried 457 hickory nuts in the fall. It found 217 of them. How many couldn't it find?

   A   S   M   D   Equation: _____

4. A dog barked seven times a minute for 15 minutes. How many times did he bark?

   A   S   M   D   Equation: _____

5. Josh ran four miles a day, every day in January. How many miles did Josh run in January?

   A   S   M   D   Equation: _____

6. The fourth-grade class left on their field trip at 8:20. They returned at 11:30. How long was their field trip?

   A   S   M   D   Equation: _____

7. Sheena filled 18 bags with popcorn. She put six ounces of popcorn in each bag. How many ounces of popcorn did she put in bags?

   A   S   M   D   Equation: _____

8. Trevor gave the clerk a ten-dollar bill. The clerk gave him $3.05 back. How much did Trevor spend?

   A   S   M   D   Equation: _____

Name: _____ Date: _____

Identify missing operational signs

Level: | 4 | 5 | 6 | 7 | 8 |

What's Missing?

Directions: Fill in the missing math symbol on each sign.

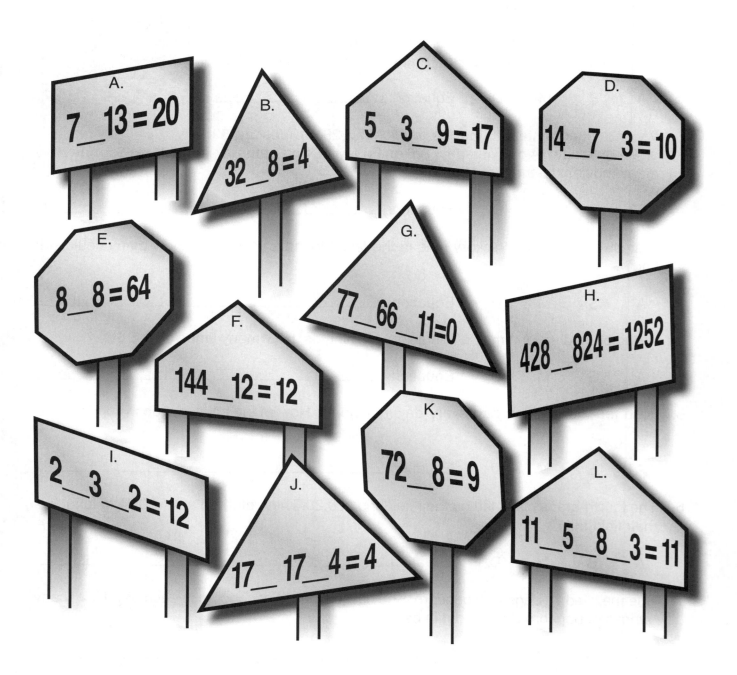

A. $7 \_\_ 13 = 20$

B. $32 \_\_ 8 = 4$

C. $5 \_\_ 3 \_\_ 9 = 17$

D. $14 \_\_ 7 \_\_ 3 = 10$

E. $8 \_\_ 8 = 64$

F. $144 \_\_ 12 = 12$

G. $77 \_\_ 66 \_\_ 11 = 0$

H. $428 \_\_ 824 = 1252$

I. $2 \_\_ 3 \_\_ 2 = 12$

J. $17 \_\_ 17 \_\_ 4 = 4$

K. $72 \_\_ 8 = 9$

L. $11 \_\_ 5 \_\_ 8 \_\_ 3 = 11$

Today's Riddle: What has three feet, but no toes?

Name: _____ Date: _____

Show relationship between multiplication and division   **Level:** | 4 | 5 | 6 | 7 | 8 |

Finish the Fact Families

Directions: Fill in the missing numbers. The first one has been done for you.

A.
8 x 2 = 16
2 x 8 = 16
16 ÷ 8 = 2
16 ÷ 2 = 8

B.
7 x ___ = 21
___ x 7 = 21
21 ÷ 7 = ___
21 ÷ ___ = 7

C.
9 x ___ = 54
___ x 9 = 54
54 ÷ 9 = ___
54 ÷ ___ = 9

D.
4 x 5 = ___
5 x ___ = 20
20 ÷ ___ = 5
20 ÷ ___ = 4

E.
11 x ___ = 66
___ x 11 = 66
66 ÷ 11 = ___
66 ÷ ___ = 11

F.
3 x ___ = 24
___ x 3 = 24
24 ÷ 3 = ___
24 ÷ ___ = 3

G.
8 x ___ = 72
___ x ___ = 72
72 ÷ ___ = ___
72 ÷ ___ = ___

H.
___ x 8 = 56
___ x ___ = 56
56 ÷ ___ = ___
56 ÷ ___ = ___

I.
6 x ___ = 48
___ x ___ = 48
48 ÷ ___ = ___
48 ÷ ___ = ___

J.
6 x ___ = 42
___ x ___ = 42
42 ÷ ___ = ___
42 ÷ ___ = ___

K.
7 x ___ = 63
___ x ___ = 63
63 ÷ ___ = ___
63 ÷ ___ = ___

L.
5 x ___ = 60
___ x ___ = 60
60 ÷ ___ = ___
60 ÷ ___ = ___

M.
___ x 3 = 12
___ x ___ = 12
12 ÷ ___ = ___
12 ÷ ___ = ___

N.
___ x 9 = 45
___ x ___ = 45
45 ÷ ___ = ___
45 ÷ ___ = ___

O.
9 x ___ = 99
___ x ___ = 99
99 ÷ ___ = ___
99 ÷ ___ = ___

Name: _____ Date: _____

Identify Processes

Level: | 5 | 6 | 7 | 8 |

Mystery Squares

Directions: Add? Subtract? Multiply? Divide? Discover which operation solves each square. Then finish each square. HINT: Start with the number in the left-most box in the top row, and perform some operation together with the number diagonally across from it in the left-hand column.

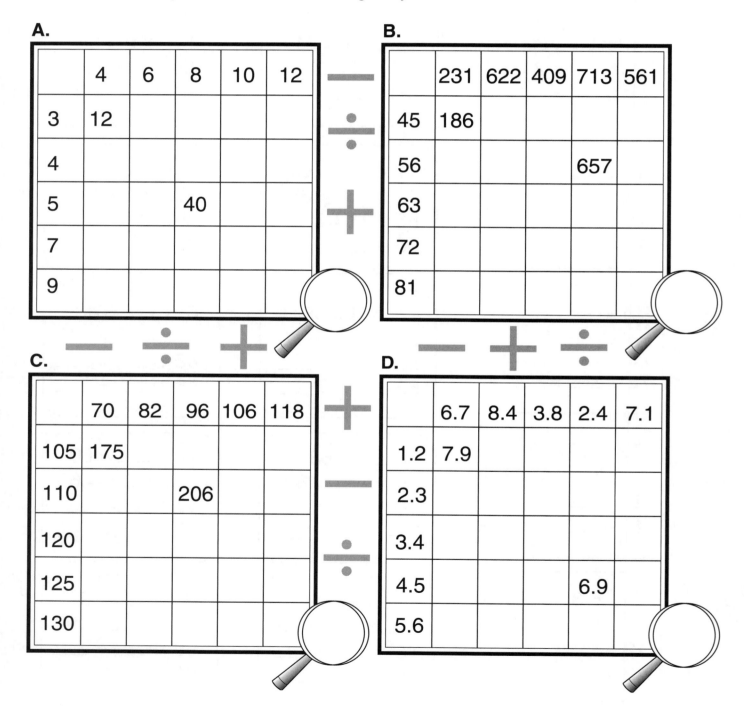

A.

	4	6	8	10	12
3	12				
4					
5			40		
7					
9					

B.

	231	622	409	713	561
45	186				
56				657	
63					
72					
81					

C.

	70	82	96	106	118
105	175				
110			206		
120					
125					
130					

D.

	6.7	8.4	3.8	2.4	7.1
1.2	7.9				
2.3					
3.4					
4.5				6.9	
5.6					

Name: _____ Date: _____

Review various operations

Level: 4 5 6 7 8

Historical Math

Directions: Find the answers to the following word problems.

A.   On July 20, 1801, a 1,235-pound wheel of cheese was pressed at the farm of Elisha Brown, Jr. The huge wheel of cheese was later loaded onto a horse-drawn wagon and presented to President Thomas Jefferson at the White House. How many 6-ounce pieces of cheese could have been cut from the giant cheese wheel?

_____

B.   A minimum wage of 40 cents per hour was established on July 12, 1933. How much would a worker have made for 40 hours a week at minimum wage?

_____

C.   On July 22, 1933, aviator Wiley Post ended his first around-the-world flight in his famous plane, the "Winnie Mae." He traveled 15,596 miles in 7 days, 18 hours, and 45 minutes. What was his average speed?

_____

D.   John Sigmund of St. Louis, Missouri, completed a 292-mile swim down the Mississippi River on July 29, 1940. It took him 89 hours and 48 minutes to swim from St. Louis to Caruthersville, Missouri, without stopping. What was his average speed?

_____

E.   On August 1, 1894, George Samuelson and Frank Harbo completed a 3,000-mile journey across the Atlantic Ocean in a rowboat. They landed in England, after having left New York on June 6th. Counting the day they left and the day they arrived, how many days did the trip take?

_____

F.   Lou Dillon became the first American racehorse to break the two-minute mile barrier on August 24, 1903. He galloped to a win at Readville, Maine, in 1 minute, 58.5 seconds. How fast did he run?

_____

G.   The Dow Jones Industrial Average closed at 2635.84 after a gain of 43.84 points on August 10, 1937. What was the Dow Jones Industrial Average at the beginning of that day?

_____

Name: _____   Date: _____

Solve equations using various operations

Level: 4 5 6 7 8

Body Math

Directions: Use the information below to answer the questions.

The average person's heart beats 103,680 times a day.

A.   How many heartbeats is that per minute? _____

Take your pulse for 15 seconds after exercising strenuously for 10 minutes. Multiply by four to get your rate per minute.

B.   What was your pulse rate? _____

Take your pulse for 15 seconds after resting for 10 minutes.

C.   What was your pulse rate? _____

Human blood travels about 61,320 miles in a year.

D.   How far does it travel in one day? _____

E.   In one hour? _____

Human hair grows at a rate of about 0.5 inches per month.

F.   If your hair were 5 inches long now, about how many months would it take for it to be 21 inches long?

_____

In May 1992, the hair of a woman in Massachusetts measured 12 feet 2 inches long.

G.   How long would it take to grow hair that long? _____

Fingernails grow at a rate of about 1/25 inch per week—four times faster than toenails. In 1992, a man in India had one fingernail that was 40 inches long.

H.   About how long did it take for that fingernail to grow? _____

Did You Know? It takes only 17 facial muscles to smile, but it takes 43 muscles to frown.

Name: _____ Date: _____

Add four numbers   **Level:** | 4 | 5 | 6 | 7 | 8 |

At the End of the Rainbow

Directions: Each pot of gold contains four numbers. Add them up and write the total at the top.

Example:

20

6 4
3 7

A.

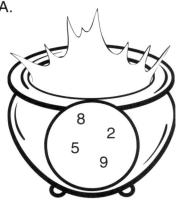

8
  2
5
  9

B.

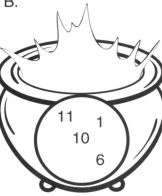

11 1
  10
    6

C.

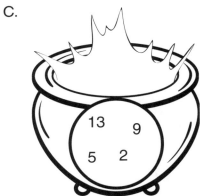

13 9
5 2

D.

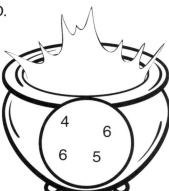

4 6
6 5

E.

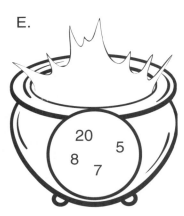

20 5
8 7

F.

40
30 10
20

G.

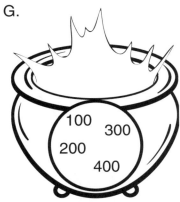

100
  300
200
  400

H.

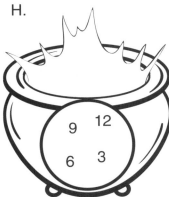

9 12
6 3

Today's Riddle: If two is company and three is a crowd, what are four and five?

Name: _____ Date: _____

Add five numbers

Level: 4 5 6 7 8

Up, Up, and Away

1. You will need colored pencils and two decks of cards, aces through tens. Each player needs a copy of this page.

2. Shuffle and place cards face down.

3. All players draw five cards and add up the total. (Aces count as 1.)

4. Players check each other's addition. The player with the highest total colors one section of his or her hot air balloon.

5. Discard and draw five new cards each time. If you run out of cards, reshuffle and start over.

6. The first player to color all sections of a balloon wins.

Name: _____ Date: _____

Calculate temperature/Complete the chart

Level: | 4 | 5 | 6 | 7 | 8 |

Cricket Math

Male crickets produce chirping noises by rubbing their front wings together. The warmer the temperature, the faster they chirp. If it's between 45 and 80 degrees Fahrenheit, you can tell the exact temperature by counting the number of chirps in 15 seconds and adding 37.

A.   A cricket chirped 18 times in 15 seconds on July 4. What was the temperature?

_____

B.   A cricket chirped 96 times in one minute on July 5. What was the temperature?

_____

C.   How much warmer was it on July 5 than on July 4? _____

D.   On July 6, the temperature was 65 degrees. How many times did the cricket chirp in 15 seconds?

_____

E.   Complete the chart.

Temperature	# of Chirps	Temperature	# of Chirps
	8	46	
	13	49	
	17	53	
	19	58	
	23	64	
	26	69	
	29	70	
	30	72	
	35	75	
	36	77	
	39	79	
	42	80	

Name: _____ Date: _____

Subtract numbers up to 12   **Level:** ` 4   5   6   7   8 `

A Long Way Down

300

300

Directions: You will need pencils and two dice to play.

Players take turns rolling the dice.

First turn: Subtract the number rolled from the number at the top of the ladder. Write the answer on the next rung down.

Second turn: Roll dice and subtract the number rolled from the number on the second rung.

Continue down the ladder, rolling the dice and subtracting.

When both players get to the bottom of the ladder, the one with the lowest total wins.

Players should check each other's subtraction for accuracy.

Today's Riddle: How many ladders would it take to reach the sun?

Name: _____   Date: _____

Use a number line   **Level:** | 4 | 5 | 6 | 7 | 8 |

Hot and Cold

A.   How are thermometers like number lines? _____

_____

Directions: Calculate the difference in temperature between each pair of thermometers below.

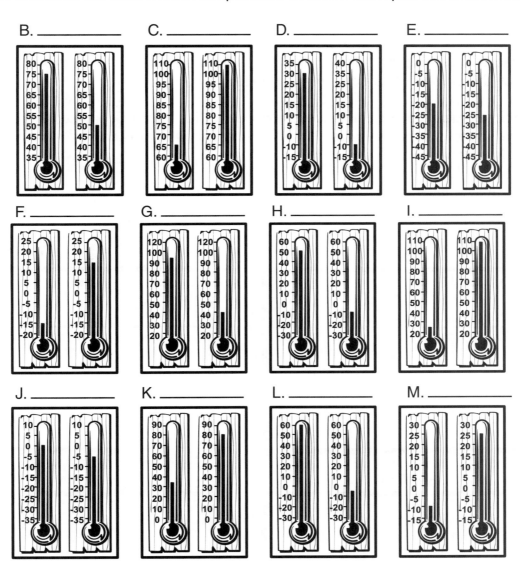

B. _____ C. _____ D. _____ E. _____

F. _____ G. _____ H. _____ I. _____

J. _____ K. _____ L. _____ M. _____

Something to think about: If it's zero degrees outside today, and it's supposed to be twice as cold tomorrow, how cold will it be?

Name: _____ Date: _____

Review subtraction

Tic-Tac-Subtract

1. You will need several game markers for each player (two different colors) and two dice.

2. Players prepare a game board by taking turns writing any number between 50 and 100 in the boxes on the game board in any order.

3. Players take turns pointing to any box without a game marker on it and rolling the dice.

4. The player subtracts the number on the dice from the number in the box. If the answer is correct, the player puts a game marker on that box.

5. If the answer is incorrect, the player skips a turn. Players check each other's answers. The first person to cover three boxes in a row wins. Game boards can be reused or new ones made for each game.

Example: A player points to a box with a 77 and rolls a 9. If the answer given is 68, that player covers the box with a marker.

Game 1

Game 2

Game 3

Game 4

Name: _____ Date: _____

Review multiplication facts

Level: | 4 | 5 | 6 | 7 | 8 |

Multiplication Bingo

Materials:

> One Bingo card for each player (Additional cards may be made by the teacher or students.)
> One deck of cards: ace through 10 (ace = 1)
> Markers

To play:

1. The caller shuffles the deck and draws two cards.
2. The caller announces the numbers on the cards.
3. Players multiply the two numbers and mark a square on the Bingo card with that answer.
4. If the correct answer is not on the card, no square is marked.
5. The caller draws two more cards, and play continues.
6. The caller records the answers of all pairs.
7. The first player to cover five squares in a row in any direction wins, if his/her answers match those recorded by the caller.

9	48	25	3	70
64	15	40	45	30
27	35	Free	72	54
42	6	30	63	14
35	5	48	90	4

12	7	56	28	42
63	20	50	2	4
18	8	Free	24	36
10	25	60	81	18
16	10	49	56	54

12	6	36	8	20
1	60	15	18	30
14	64	Free	42	35
27	5	48	18	81
25	56	63	49	35

42	6	21	63	14
100	24	64	81	56
15	8	Free	20	28
36	27	48	54	45
40	3	16	25	9

Name: _____   Date: _____

Recognize multiples of 3, 5, 7, 9, and 11

Level: 4 5 6 7 8

Multiple Multiples

1. Circle each multiple of 3.
2. Put a triangle around each multiple of 5.
3. Color each multiple of 7 green.
4. Color each multiple of 11 red.
5. Put an X on each multiple of 9.

1	2	3	4	5	6	7	8	9	10
11	12	13	14	15	16	17	18	19	20
21	22	23	24	25	26	27	28	29	30
31	32	33	34	35	36	37	38	39	40
41	42	43	44	45	46	47	48	49	50
51	52	53	54	55	56	57	58	59	60
61	62	63	64	65	66	67	68	69	70
71	72	73	74	75	76	77	78	79	80
81	82	83	84	85	86	87	88	89	90
91	92	93	94	95	96	97	98	99	100

A.   What numbers are multiples of both 3 and 5? _____

_____

B.   What numbers are multiples of both 7 and 11? _____

_____

C.   What numbers are multiples of both 9 and 11? _____

_____

D.   What numbers are multiples common to all of the numbers 3, 5, 7, 9, and 11?

_____

Name: _____ Date: _____

Multiply three numbers

Level: | 4 | 5 | 6 | 7 | 8 |

Going Buggy

You will need colored pencils, scrap paper, 3″ x 5″ index cards, and a deck of playing cards (only cards two through ten).

1. Shuffle and place cards facedown.

2. All players draw three cards and multiply the three numbers.

    Card 1 x Card 2 x Card 3 = ?

3. Players check each other's multiplication. The player with the highest total draws one section of an imaginary insect on his or her index card.

4. Discard and draw three new playing cards each time. If you run out of cards, reshuffle and continue.

5. Each insect must have three body parts, six legs, two antennae, two eyes, and a mouth. The first player to complete an imaginary bug wins the round.

6. Name your insects and display them for others to enjoy.

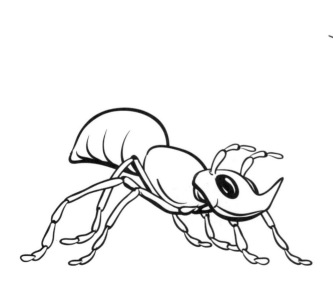

Name: _____ Date: _____

Multiplication of positive and negative integers

Level: 5 6 7 8

The Multiplying Maid

  This card game is for 2 or 3 players. Use a regular deck of 52 cards with the addition of the two jokers. Each ace in the deck represents the number one, and each numbered card two through ten represents that number, respectively. Each jack represents the number zero, each queen represents the number eleven, each king represents the number twelve, and each joker represents the number fifteen. The black cards all represent positive numbers, the red cards all represent negative numbers, and the jokers are both positive.

1. One player acts as the dealer. After shuffling the deck, each player is dealt an equal supply of cards face-down. Any player can re-shuffle this pile at any time, provided he/she does not *peek* at the cards in the pile.

2. Play starts by each player turning over the top two cards from his/her pile. Each player, in turn, calls out the product of the two numbers that the two cards represent. The player with the highest product takes all of the cards from the round of play and puts them into his/her pile.

3. If there is a two-way tie for highest product, then those two players must turn over two more cards face-up. The one with the higher product of all four cards now facing up wins all of the cards that have been turned face-up during this round of play, including those from the player not involved in the tie.

4. If all three players tie for the high product, then all three players turn over two more cards face-up, and the player with the highest product of all four cards wins all of the cards facing up during the entire round of play.

5. Rounds of play continue in this manner until one player collects all of the cards or until the other players do not have enough cards to either start or finish any round of play. If one player does not have enough cards to play—that is, only one card left—then that card is put into the pot for that round, and that player is finished for that game.

  A variation of this game can be accomplished by using two entire decks, plus jokers, so that 4 or 6 players can play simultaneously. If you want to allow five players to start the same game, then you will need to use two decks and two extra jokers for a total of 110 cards, which includes 6 jokers.

  Other variations would include assigning different values to the cards so that different products will come into play. Another variation is turning up three cards to determine products during the original play for each round, and using only one extra card for each player involved in a tie. You can also use addition of the face-up cards as the mechanism to play the game. Also, you can have the winner of each round be the player with the smallest product or sum. Experiment and find out what is the most fun and entertaining for your class or study group!

Name: _____   Date: _____

Practice short division skills,
with and without remainders

Level: | 4 | 5 | 6 | 7 | 8 |

Dino Division

Materials: You will need a pencil and a colored pencil for each player, one die, and the Dino Division game board below. Each player needs a different color pencil.

Directions:
1. First player rolls the die.
2. Player divides the number shown on any segment of the dinosaur by the number on the die and writes the answer, including the remainder, if any.

3. If the answer is correct, the player colors that part of the dinosaur.
4. If the answer is incorrect, the opponent colors in that part and takes a turn.
5. When all sections are colored, the player with the most colored sections wins.

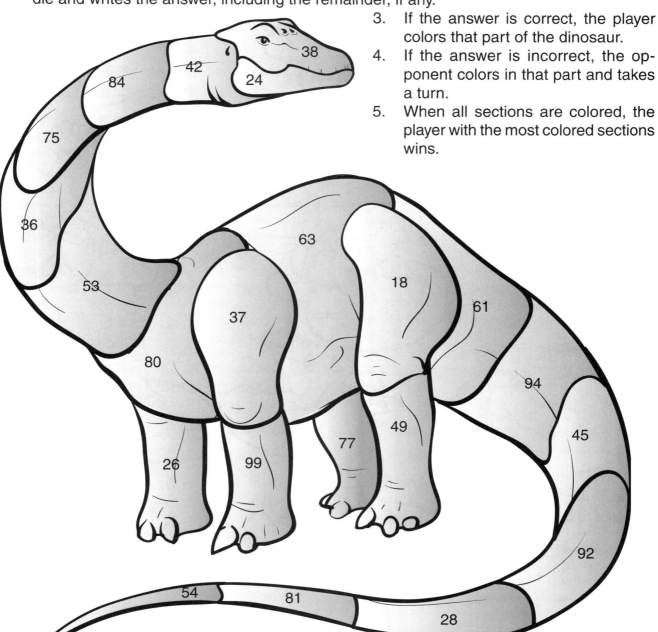

Name: _____   Date: _____

Write division equations to match answers given   **Level:** | 4 | 5 | 6 | 7 | 8 |

Hop to It

Directions: Rearrange the digits in the frogs and write them in the lily pads to get the correct answers.

A. 721   ____ ÷ ____ = 3

B. 416   ____ ÷ ____ = 4

C. 456   ____ ÷ ____ = 9

D. 603   ____ ÷ ____ = 5

E. 567   ____ ÷ ____ = 8

F. 274   ____ ÷ ____ = 6

G. 369   ____ ÷ ____ = 7

H. 864   ____ ÷ ____ = 8

I. 436   ____ ÷ ____ = 9

J. 482   ____ ÷ ____ = 7

K. 279   ____ ÷ ____ = 3

L. 642   ____ ÷ ____ = 4

M. 459   ____ ÷ ____ = 6

N. 504   ____ ÷ ____ = 8

O. 553   ____ ÷ ____ = 7

Name: _____ Date: _____

Divide two-digit numbers by one-digit numbers

Level: 4 5 6 7 8

Leftovers

1. You will need two decks of cards, 2 through 9. Each player will need scrap paper, a pencil, and 15 small game markers of one color (different color for each player).

2. Players take turns drawing three cards and arranging them like this:

3. Divide to find the quotient and remainder. If the answer is correct, place a game marker on a container in the refrigerator below with the same number as the remainder. If no container with that number remains, skip a turn.

4. When all containers are covered with markers, the person with the most game pieces on containers wins.

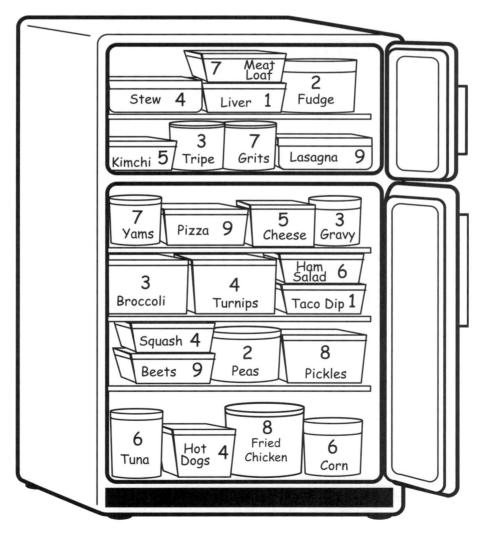

Name: _____ Date: _____

Divide four-digit numbers by one- and two-digit numbers **Level:** 4 5 6 7 8

Find a Penny

Find a penny, pick it up.
All day long you'll have good luck.

1. You will need two dice, scrap paper, and pencils. Each player needs a different-colored colored pencil.

2. The first player rolls the dice, divides the date on the first penny by the number rolled, and gives the answer, including remainder, if any.

3. Use scrap paper to find the answers. Players check each other's answers.

4. If the answer is correct, the player colors in that penny. If not, the player skips a turn. Players continue taking turns until all pennies are colored. The one with the most pennies wins.

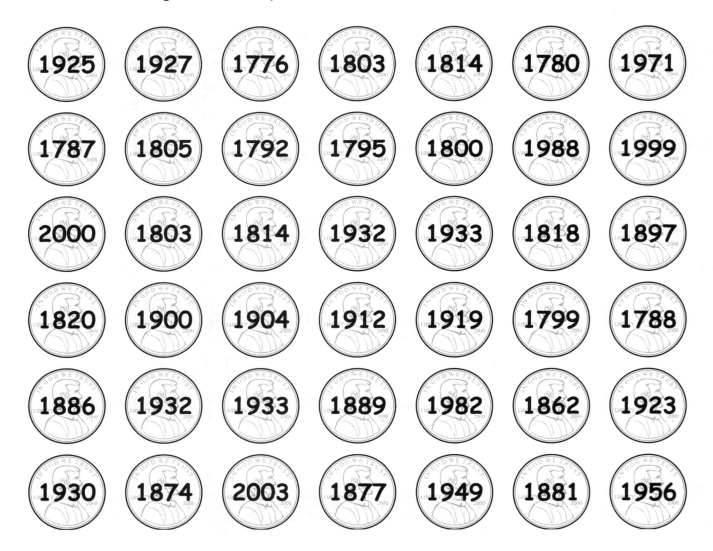

Name: _____ Date: _____

Review division

Level: | 4 | 5 | 6 | 7 | 8 |

No Remainders

Directions: You will need a regular black pencil and a red and a green colored pencil.

A. Circle all numbers that can be divided evenly by 3.

B. Put a triangle around all numbers that can be divided evenly by 8.

C. Color all numbers green that can be divided evenly by 7.

D. Color all numbers red that can be divided evenly by 5.

E. Put an X on all numbers that can be divided evenly by more than one of the above numbers.

F. What numbers can be divided evenly by both 5 and 7? _____

G. What numbers can be divided evenly by both 8 and 3? _____

H. What numbers can be divided evenly by all four numbers: 3, 5, 7, and 8? _____

1	2	3	4	5	6	7	8	9	10
11	12	13	14	15	16	17	18	19	20
21	22	23	24	25	26	27	28	29	30
31	32	33	34	35	36	37	38	39	40
41	42	43	44	45	46	47	48	49	50
51	52	53	54	55	56	57	58	59	60
61	62	63	64	65	66	67	68	69	70
71	72	73	74	75	76	77	78	79	80
81	82	83	84	85	86	87	88	89	90
91	92	93	94	95	96	97	98	99	100

Name: _____ Date: _____

Review division with remainders

Level: | 4 | 5 | 6 | 7 | 8

With Remainders

You will need scrap paper, pencils, and a deck of cards (only cards 2 through 10), and each player will need a different color of colored pencil.

1. Players take turns drawing two cards and writing a division question in this format.
    "What numbers can be divided by ... (the higher number) and leave a remainder equal to ... (the lower number)?"
    Example: Player draws a 10 and a 2 and writes: What numbers can be divided by 10 with a remainder of 2?
2. If a player draws a pair, discard one card and draw a new card.
3. Player writes all answers on scrap paper and colors all numbers below that are correct. Players check each other's answers.
4. Only correct answers may be colored. If a player misses some answers, the other player can claim those numbers and color them.
5. When all numbers are colored or when the time limit is up, the player with the most colored numbers wins.

	2	3	4	5	6	7	8	9	10
11	12	13	14	15	16	17	18	19	20
21	22	23	24	25	26	27	28	29	30
31	32	33	34	35	36	37	38	39	40
41	42	43	44	45	46	47	48	49	50
51	52	53	54	55	56	57	58	59	60
61	62	63	64	65	66	67	68	69	70
71	72	73	74	75	76	77	78	79	80
81	82	83	84	85	86	87	88	89	90
91	92	93	94	95	96	97	98	99	

Name: _____ Date: _____

Identify/discriminate between types of fractions

Level: 4 5 6 7 8

Fraction Collections

Tori, Taj, and Devan collect fraction cards. Their cards are all mixed up and need to be sorted.

Tori collects only proper fractions. (Examples: $\frac{1}{3}$, $\frac{5}{6}$) Color Tori's fractions blue.

Taj collects only improper fractions. (Examples: $\frac{9}{5}$, $\frac{4}{3}$) Color Taj's fractions red.

Devan collects only mixed numbers. (Examples: $1\frac{7}{8}$, $2\frac{1}{4}$) Color Devan's fractions green.

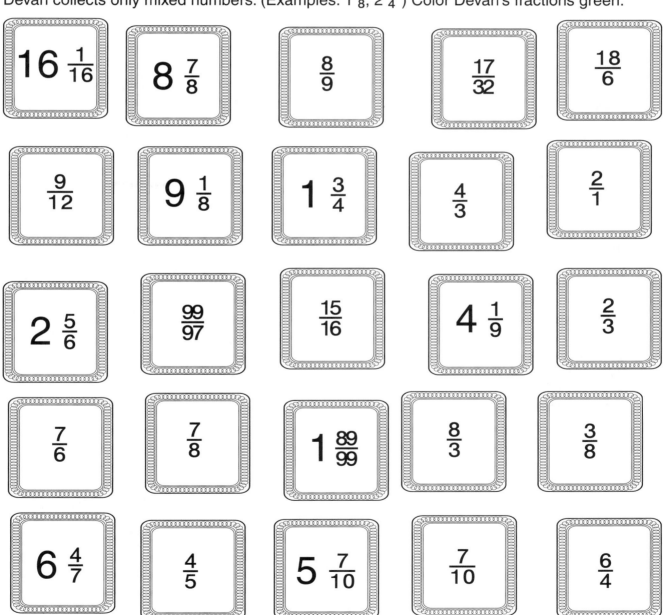

$16\frac{1}{16}$ $8\frac{7}{8}$ $\frac{8}{9}$ $\frac{17}{32}$ $\frac{18}{6}$

$\frac{9}{12}$ $9\frac{1}{8}$ $1\frac{3}{4}$ $\frac{4}{3}$ $\frac{2}{1}$

$2\frac{5}{6}$ $\frac{99}{97}$ $\frac{15}{16}$ $4\frac{1}{9}$ $\frac{2}{3}$

$\frac{7}{6}$ $\frac{7}{8}$ $1\frac{89}{99}$ $\frac{8}{3}$ $\frac{3}{8}$

$6\frac{4}{7}$ $\frac{4}{5}$ $5\frac{7}{10}$ $\frac{7}{10}$ $\frac{6}{4}$

Math Skills Mind Benders

Fractions, Decimals, and Percents: Balancing Act

Name: _____ Date: _____

Convert fractions to decimals/
Convert decimals to fractions

Level: | 4 | 5 | 6 | 7 | 8 |

Balancing Act

Directions: Write the equivalent fractions to balance the scales.

A.

B.

C.

D.

Directions: Write the equivalent decimals to balance the scales.

E.

F.

G.

H.

Name: _____ Date: _____

Add and subtract fractions

Level: | 4 | 5 | 6 | 7 | 8 |

Bull's-eye

Directions: Take the fraction in the bull's-eye and add each fraction in the next ring. Place the answers in the outer ring. One has been done for you as an example in each bull's-eye.

A. B.

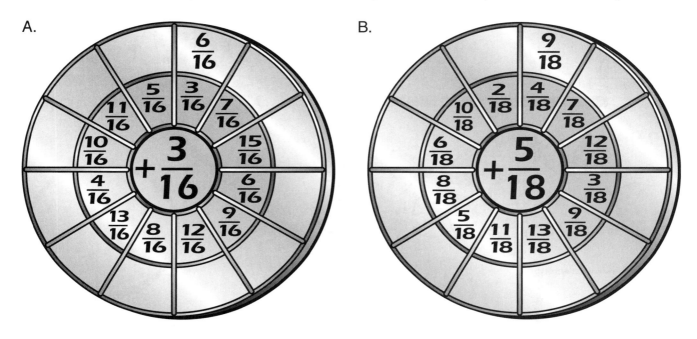

Directions: Take the fraction in the bull's-eye and subtract each fraction in the next ring. Place the answers in the outer ring. One has been done for you as an example.

C. D.

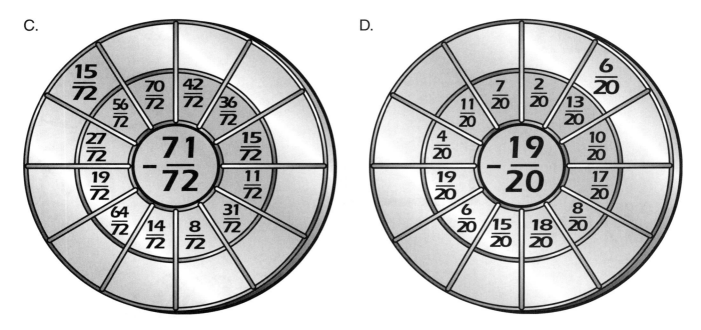

Name: _____ Date: _____

Create pictorial equivalents of decimals

Level: | 4 | 5 | 6 | 7 | 8 |

Show Me

Directions: Use colored pencils to shade in the decimal or fraction part of the object.

A. **0.6**

B. **0.2**

C. **0.9**

D. **0.5**

E. $\frac{1}{10}$

F. **0.7**

G. **0.8**

H. **0.7**

I. **0.3**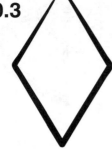

J. $\frac{5}{10}$

Name: _____   Date: _____

Convert improper fractions to mixed numbers

Level: | 4 | 5 | 6 | 7 | 8 |

Sock Sort

Directions: For each pair of socks, convert the improper fraction in the first sock to a mixed number. Write the mixed number in the second sock. Reduce fractions to lowest terms.

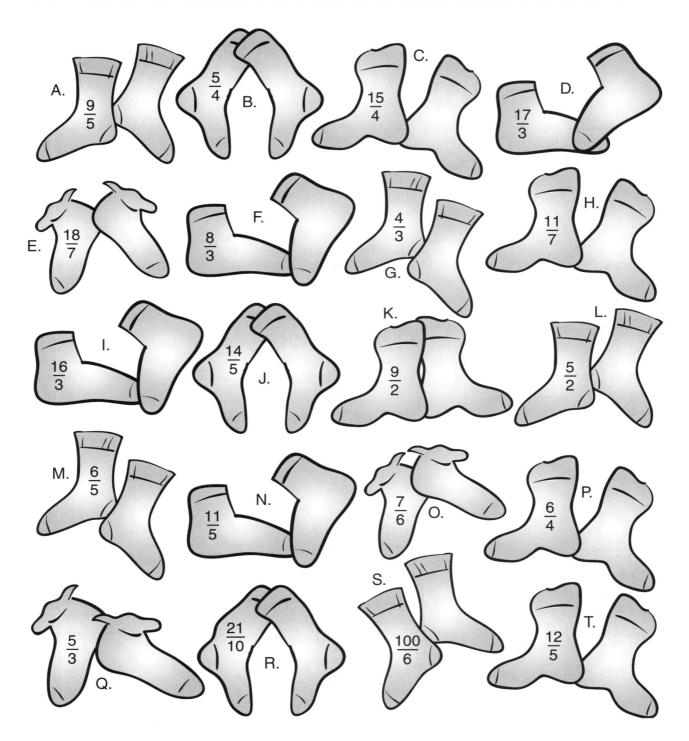

A. $\frac{9}{5}$

B. $\frac{5}{4}$

C. $\frac{15}{4}$

D. $\frac{17}{3}$

E. $\frac{18}{7}$

F. $\frac{8}{3}$

G. $\frac{4}{3}$

H. $\frac{11}{7}$

I. $\frac{16}{3}$

J. $\frac{14}{5}$

K. $\frac{9}{2}$

L. $\frac{5}{2}$

M. $\frac{6}{5}$

N. $\frac{11}{5}$

O. $\frac{7}{6}$

P. $\frac{6}{4}$

Q. $\frac{5}{3}$

R. $\frac{21}{10}$

S. $\frac{100}{6}$

T. $\frac{12}{5}$

Name: _____ Date: _____

Ordering and adding fractions

Level: 4 5 6 7 8

Ordering and Adding

Directions: Number the circles from 1 to 8 according to the size of the shaded area. Write 1 for the circle with the smallest amount shaded and 8 for the circle with the largest amount shaded.

A. _____ B. _____ C. _____ D. _____

E. _____ F. _____ G. _____ H. _____

Directions: Add the shaded amounts of the shapes in each row. Reduce answers to lowest terms.

I. 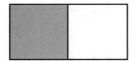 + 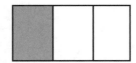 = _____

J.   +   = _____

K.   +   = _____

L.   +   = _____

M.   +   = _____

Name: _____ Date: _____

Convert decimals, mixed numbers, and improper fractions to lowest terms

Level: | 4 | 5 | 6 | 7 | 8 |

Apple Picking

1. You will need two dice. Each player needs a pencil and scrap paper.

2. All players roll two dice. The player with the highest total selects one apple on the tree and finds the equivalent fraction on another apple on the ground. If correct, the player writes his or her initials on both apples.

3. All players roll each time. Only the player with the highest number gets a turn. Continue until all apples are matched. The player with the most apples wins.

Convert numbers to fractions, decimals, and ratios   **Level:** | 4 | 5 | 6 | 7 | 8 |

Alien Survey

Directions: Write each answer as a fraction, a decimal, and a ratio. Reduce fractions to lowest terms.

Example: Seven out of ten aliens said they liked peanut butter better than jelly.

Fraction: $\frac{7}{10}$ Decimal: 0.7   Ratio: 7:10

A.   Four out of ten aliens had six arms.

Fraction: _____   Decimal: _____   Ratio: _____

B.   Three out of ten aliens liked rock music better than polkas.

Fraction: _____   Decimal: _____   Ratio: _____

C.   Six out of ten aliens could not swim.

Fraction: _____   Decimal: _____   Ratio: _____

D.   Six out of twelve aliens were afraid of flying.

Fraction: _____   Decimal: _____   Ratio: _____

E.   Twenty-five out of 100 aliens liked chocolate milk better than prune juice.

Fraction: _____   Decimal: _____   Ratio: _____

F.   Thirteen out of 100 aliens liked Earthlings better than Martians.

Fraction: _____   Decimal: _____   Ratio: _____

G.   Four out of sixteen aliens had never been to Pluto.

Fraction: _____   Decimal: _____   Ratio: _____

H.   Nine out of twelve aliens preferred catsup to mustard on their cereal.

Fraction: _____   Decimal: _____   Ratio: _____

I.   Of 1,000 aliens surveyed, 350 liked pizza more than oatmeal.

Fraction: _____   Decimal: _____   Ratio: _____

Name: _____ Date: _____

Calculate percent/Rounding

Level: 4 5 6 7 8

Big Tippers

Directions: Before he or she paid the bill, each customer left a tip at the table. Using the total of each bill and the percent each person tipped, calculate the amount each left for a tip, and write it in the chart below. Round your answers to the nearest cent.

	Total Bill	Percent of Tip	Total Tip
A.	$10.44	15%	
B.	$27.90	14%	
C.	$16.71	16%	
D.	$18.77	9%	
E.	$15.82	10%	
F.	$21.04	17%	
G.	$14.97	11%	
H.	$9.36	13%	
I.	$19.47	12%	
J.	$31.64	8%	

Name: _____ Date: _____

Calculate percent/Find total cost/Rounding

Level: ▮▮▮ 5 6 7 8

Tax on Tacks

Directions: Find the amount of sales tax on each item. Calculate the total cost of the item with tax. Round answers to the nearest cent.

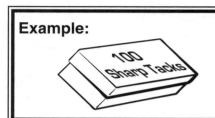

Example:

Price: $1.49

Tax: 5%

Amount of tax: $0.07

Total cost: $1.56

A.

Price: $9.99

Tax: 4%

Amount of tax: _____

Total cost: _____

E.

Price: $17.38

Tax: 7%

Amount of tax: _____

Total cost: _____

B.

Price: $129.86

Tax: 6%

Amount of tax: _____

Total cost: _____

F.

Price: $1.98

Tax: 4.5%

Amount of tax: _____

Total cost: _____

C.

Price: $773.68

Tax: 5%

Amount of tax: _____

Total cost: _____

G.

Price: $68.25

Tax: 5.5%

Amount of tax: _____

Total cost: _____

D.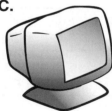

Price: $29.95

Tax: 6%

Amount of tax: _____

Total cost: _____

H.

Price: $21,579

Tax: 6%

Amount of tax: _____

Total cost: _____

Fractions, Decimals, and Percents: At the Factor-E

Name: _____ Date: _____

Discover least common denominator **Level:** 4 5 6 7 8

At the Factor-E

The **least common denominator** is the lowest number that is evenly divisible by two or more denominators.

Directions: Find the least common denominators.

A.   The least common denominator for 2 and 3 is _____.

B.   The least common denominator for 6 and 8 is _____.

C.   The least common denominator for 5 and 9 is _____.

D.   The least common denominator

    for 6 and 9 is _____.

E.   The least common denominator

    for 8 and 10 is _____.

F.   The least common denominator for 7 and 3 is _____.

G.   The least common denominator for 9 and 12 is _____.

H.   The least common denominator

    for 3 and 5 is _____.

I.   The least common denominator

    for 7 and 8 is _____.

J.   The least common denominator for 8 and 12 is _____.

K.   The least common denominator for 15 and 6 is _____.

Add fractions

Level: 5 6 7 8

Closest to One

You will need several decks of cards (only cards 2 through 10). Each player will need scrap paper and a pencil.

1. Deal two cards to each player, both face up.

2. The number on each card is equal to the denominator of a fraction.

   $2 = \frac{1}{2}$ $3 = \frac{1}{3}$ $4 = \frac{1}{4}$ $5 = \frac{1}{5}$, etc.

3. The object of each round is to add up your cards to equal 1 (or to get as close to 1 as possible without going over).

4. After players look at their cards and add up the fractions, they can ask for another card or pass. All cards are dealt face up.

5. The player can ask for additional cards up to a total of six and may pass after any card.

6. All players add their fraction totals. The player closest to a total of 1 without going over wins the round and earns 1 point.

7. In the case of a tie, both players earn 1 point.

8. Game ends when one player earns 10 points.

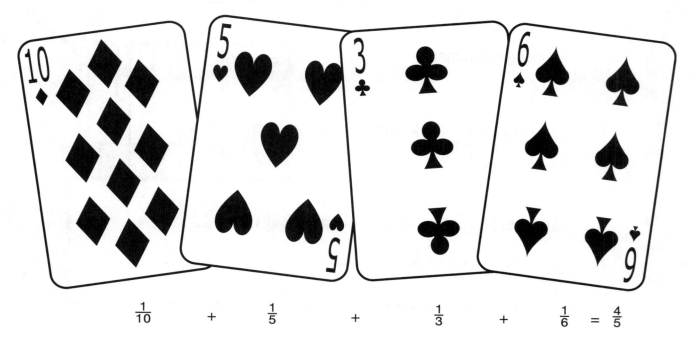

$$\frac{1}{10} \quad + \quad \frac{1}{5} \quad + \quad \frac{1}{3} \quad + \quad \frac{1}{6} \quad = \quad \frac{4}{5}$$

Name: _____ Date: _____

Subtract fractions   Level: ■ 4 5 6 7 8

Grid Work

You will need two dice, scrap paper, and a different color of colored pencil for each player.

1. Players take turns. Roll two dice, one at a time.

2. Use the first number rolled to locate the coordinate on the left side of the grid and the second number for the coordinate along the bottom of the grid. Find the box described by the two coordinates.

   Example: If you shook a 6, then a 2, you would go to the box with the equation $\frac{3}{4} - \frac{2}{3} =$.

3. Solve the equation in the box. Reduce fractions to lowest terms. If the answer is correct, the player then colors in the box.

4. If that equation is already solved, play passes to the next player.

5. The player with the most boxes colored wins the game.

	1	2	3	4	5	6
6	$\frac{1}{2} - \frac{2}{6} =$	$\frac{3}{4} - \frac{2}{3} =$	$\frac{3}{8} - \frac{1}{4} =$	$\frac{2}{7} - \frac{1}{8} =$	$\frac{5}{9} - \frac{1}{3} =$	$\frac{11}{12} - \frac{3}{4} =$
5	$\frac{7}{15} - \frac{2}{5} =$	$\frac{7}{18} - \frac{2}{9} =$	$\frac{1}{3} - \frac{1}{4} =$	$\frac{7}{8} - \frac{3}{4} =$	$\frac{1}{5} - \frac{1}{10} =$	$\frac{2}{3} - \frac{1}{4} =$
4	$\frac{7}{9} - \frac{1}{3} =$	$\frac{7}{19} - \frac{1}{3} =$	$\frac{11}{12} - \frac{5}{6} =$	$\frac{3}{4} - \frac{1}{3} =$	$\frac{3}{5} - \frac{1}{10} =$	$\frac{5}{6} - \frac{1}{2} =$
3	$\frac{3}{5} - \frac{1}{3} =$	$\frac{5}{6} - \frac{1}{2} =$	$\frac{8}{9} - \frac{2}{18} =$	$\frac{7}{10} - \frac{2}{5} =$	$\frac{7}{16} - \frac{1}{3} =$	$\frac{9}{16} - \frac{1}{4} =$
2	$\frac{11}{16} - \frac{1}{2} =$	$\frac{5}{8} - \frac{1}{4} =$	$\frac{4}{5} - \frac{1}{2} =$	$\frac{13}{15} - \frac{4}{5} =$	$\frac{5}{19} - \frac{1}{10} =$	$\frac{9}{16} - \frac{2}{5} =$
1	$\frac{2}{3} - \frac{3}{6} =$	$\frac{13}{16} - \frac{5}{8} =$	$\frac{9}{10} - \frac{3}{5} =$	$\frac{7}{12} - \frac{5}{14} =$	$\frac{7}{8} - \frac{3}{4} =$	$\frac{1}{2} - \frac{3}{8} =$

Name: _____   Date: _____

Multiply fractions   **Level:** | 5   6   7   8 |

Snakes and Snails and Puppy Dog Tails

Directions: Multiply the fractions to find the answers. Write your answers in lowest terms.

A. $\frac{1}{2}$ of the students in a class have pets. $\frac{2}{3}$ of those with pets have pet snakes.

    What fraction of the class has pet snakes? _____

B.   Tina bought $2\frac{1}{2}$ pounds of apples. She ate $\frac{1}{3}$ of the apples.

    How many pounds of apples did she eat? _____

C.   Grandma bought $2\frac{7}{8}$ pounds of chocolate. She used $\frac{1}{2}$ of it to make candy.

    How many pounds of chocolate are left? _____

D.   Multiply and then subtract: There is $\frac{1}{3}$ quart of milk left. Dana drank $\frac{1}{3}$ of it. How much milk is left? _____

E.   Multiply and then add: Jeremy's puppy's tail was $\frac{1}{3}$ of a yard long in April. By the end of June, it had grown $\frac{1}{4}$ longer.

    How long was the puppy's tail by the end of June? _____

F.   The bears at the zoo like this treat so much, the zookeeper decided to make a larger batch as a special treat. Change the following recipe to make $2\frac{1}{2}$ times the amount.

Crispy Critters

Original Amount	New Amount	Ingredient
$\frac{2}{3}$ pound	_____ pound(s)	crunchy ants
$\frac{7}{8}$ pound	_____ pound(s)	peanut shells
$1\frac{3}{4}$ pounds	_____ pound(s)	chocolate-covered crickets
$\frac{1}{8}$ pound	_____ pound(s)	snails with shells
$2\frac{3}{8}$ pounds	_____ pound(s)	honey
$\frac{4}{9}$ pound	_____ pound(s)	chopped beetles

Name: _____ Date: _____

Divide fractions

Level: 4 5 6 7 8

Web Divide

Directions: Divide the fractions and place the answers in the outer ring of the web. Reduce answers to the lowest terms. Change improper fractions to mixed numbers. Show your work on another sheet of paper. One has been completed for you as an example.

A.
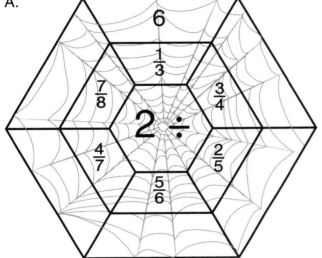

B.
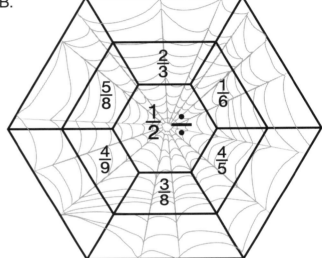

C.
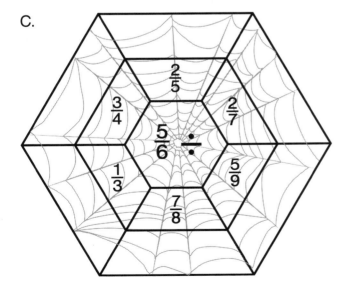

D.
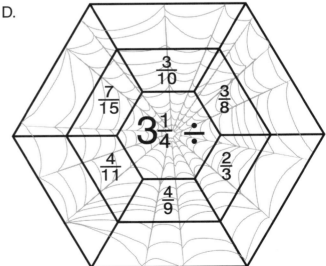

Name: _____   Date: _____

Multiply and divide fractions and decimals

Level: 4 5 6 7 8

Fraction Tic-Tac-Toe

Directions: You will need pencils and scrap paper to play this version of tic-tac-toe. It is played like regular tic-tac-toe. However, before you can put an "X" or an "O" on the board, you must solve the equation. Players check each other's answers. If incorrect, the player skips a turn.

A.

$3.5 \times 6.2 =$	$8.1 \times 7.4 =$	$0.71 \times 7.01 =$
$9\frac{1}{3} \times 7.3 =$	$5.7 \times 2\frac{1}{3} =$	$6.2 \times 4\frac{1}{2} =$
$6\frac{2}{3} \times 3.9 =$	$4.02 \times 5\frac{1}{8} =$	$8.47 \times 6.2 =$

B.

$10^4 =$	$4^3 =$	$5^2 =$
$2^6 =$	$3^6 =$	$10^3 =$
$4^4 =$	$5^3 =$	$6^3 =$

C.

$3\frac{1}{2} \times 6 =$	$2\frac{1}{4} \times 3\frac{1}{2} =$	$4 \times \frac{4}{9} =$
$8 \times 2\frac{1}{2} =$	$4 \times \frac{4}{16} =$	$5 \times \frac{7}{3} =$
$7 \times \frac{4}{9} =$	$3\frac{2}{3} \times 4\frac{3}{4} =$	$9\frac{2}{5} \times 1\frac{1}{2} =$

D.

$8 \div 2\frac{1}{2} =$	$9 \div \frac{1}{3} =$	$7 \div \frac{2}{5} =$
$6 \div \frac{3}{7} =$	$3 \div \frac{5}{6} =$	$5 \div \frac{2}{9} =$
$2 \div \frac{3}{8} =$	$4 \div \frac{1}{16} =$	$12 \div \frac{3}{5} =$

Reduce to lowest terms

E.

$\frac{17}{4} =$	$\frac{92}{20} =$	$\frac{13}{9} =$
$\frac{19}{3} =$	$\frac{24}{7} =$	$\frac{26}{8} =$
$\frac{42}{5} =$	$\frac{39}{6} =$	$\frac{41}{2} =$

F.

$3\frac{16}{4} =$	$2\frac{9}{5} =$	$4\frac{18}{3} =$
$7\frac{14}{2} =$	$5\frac{9}{5} =$	$9\frac{7}{2} =$
$1\frac{24}{3} =$	$6\frac{8}{3} =$	$8\frac{48}{12} =$

Name: _____ Date: _____

Calculate equivalent fractions, decimals, and percents **Level:** | 4 | 5 | 6 | 7 | 8 |

Music to My Ears

The high school band has 100 members. They include:

Woodwind Section
22 B-flat clarinet players
4 bass clarinet players
11 flute players
4 piccolo players
2 oboe players
1 bassoon player
7 alto saxophone players
5 tenor saxophone players
2 bass saxophone players

Brass Section
6 French horn players
9 trumpet players
4 cornet players
8 trombone players
3 tuba players

Percussion Section
5 snare drummers
2 bass drummers
1 cymbal player
3 timpani players
1 marimba/xylophone player

Directions: Show the proportion of the band members who play the instruments listed below. Write each answer as a decimal, a percent, and a fraction. Reduce all fractions to lowest terms.

A.   Members who play tenor saxophone

Percent: _____ Decimal: _____ Fraction: _____

B.   Members who play French horn

Percent: _____ Decimal: _____ Fraction: _____

C.   Cymbal players

Percent: _____ Decimal: _____ Fraction: _____

D.   Trumpet and cornet players

Percent: _____ Decimal: _____ Fraction: _____

E.   Trombone and tuba players

Percent: _____ Decimal: _____ Fraction: _____

F.   Tenor and bass saxophone players

Percent: _____ Decimal: _____ Fraction: _____

G.   Members who play woodwind instruments

Percent: _____ Decimal: _____ Fraction: _____

H.   Members who play brass instruments

Percent: _____ Decimal: _____ Fraction: _____

I.   Members of the percussion section

Percent: _____ Decimal: _____ Fraction: _____

Name: _____ Date: _____

Conversion of percents to rational fractions

Level: | 4 | 5 | 6 | 7 | 8 |

The Fraction-Spiral Game

This game is for 2 or more players and a judge. Determine an order of play. Each player then rolls a single die and can move forward that number of spaces if he/she answers correctly by converting the percent displayed in that box to a fraction in its reduced form. If your answer is not correct, then you must go back to where you started the round, and the die passes to the next player. You will need an exact roll to end the game.

120%	45%	240%	18%	12.5%	166%	55%	170%	1.5%	30%	160%
7.5%										37.5%
150%		16%	110%	40%	2.5%	8%	17.5%	275%		24%
550%		175%						133%		112.5%
60%		125%		80%	75%	12%		33%		125%
18%		70%		Finish		8.75%		66%		140%
90%		15%				25%		1%		220%
4%		180%	62.5%	5%	130%	250%		36%		22.5%
225%								22%		72%
83%	50%	10%	65%	85%	87.5%	20%	350%	200%		137.5%
										100%
								Start		35%

Name: _____ Date: _____

Discriminate Shapes/Use problem-solving skills

Level: | 4 | 5 | 6 | 7 | 8 |

Seeing Stars

Directions: After the circle collided with the square, along came the runaway triangle. BONK! After the three-way crash, they were seeing stars. Answer the following questions.

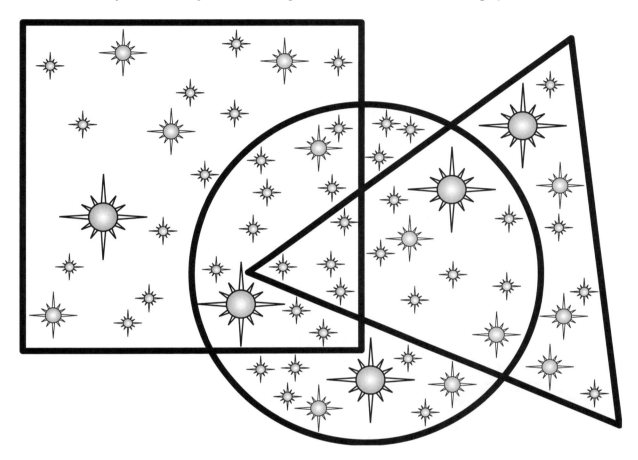

A.   How many stars are inside the square, but not in any part of the circle or triangle? _____

B.   How many stars are inside the circle, but not in any part of the triangle or square? _____

C.   How many stars are inside the area that includes the triangle and the circle, but not the square?

_____

D.   How many stars are inside the area that includes the circle and the square, but not the triangle?

_____

E.   How many stars are inside the area that includes all three figures? _____

Name: _____   Date: _____

Use manipulatives for problem-solving

Level: | 4 | 5 | 6 | 7 | 8 |

Cookie Caper

Grandma baked chocolate chip cookies and set six of them out in this pattern. She told her grandson, "If you can move one cookie and create two sets with four cookies in each set, I'll give you all six cookies."

Her grandson earned all six cookies. Can you? Which cookie do you need to move and where?

_____

_____

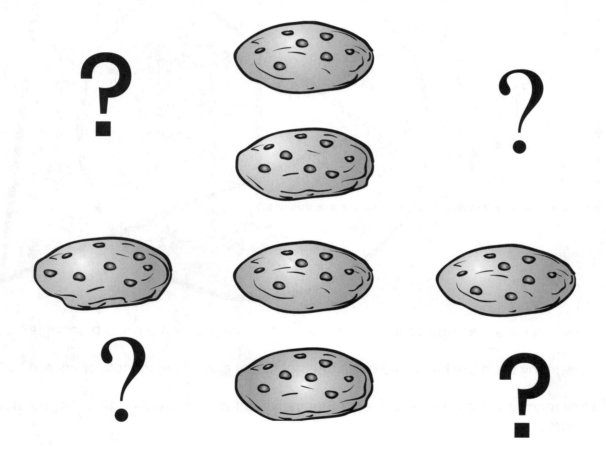

Hint: Use cookies or other objects to solve this puzzle. Set up the same pattern, then move cookies around until you figure it out. When you succeed, reward yourself with a cookie!

Today's Riddle: Grandma baked three dozen cookies. Her grandchildren ate all but eleven. How many were left?

Name: _____   Date: _____

Use manipulatives to visualize solutions   **Level:** | 4 | 5 | 6 | 7 | 8 |

Coin Tricks

Directions: Use coins to work out the answers to these coin tricks.

The twins, Julie and Jessica, each had some coins.

Julie had:

Jessica had:

Move only two coins so they both have the same amount of money.

A.   Which two coins did you move? _____

_____

B.   How much did each twin have then? _____

Aaron put a half dollar in a coin-changing machine. He received six coins equal to 50 cents.

C.   Give two possible combinations of coins he could have received.

_____

_____

How much money did Tammy have in her piggy bank on Sunday? Use the clues to find out.

   On Monday, she put in two dimes and took out four pennies.

   On Tuesday, she put in three quarters and took out a dime.

   On Wednesday, she took out a nickel and put in six pennies.

   On Thursday, she took out seven cents and put in two nickels.

   On Friday, she took out all of her money: 99 cents.

D.   How much money had been in Tammy's bank on Sunday? _____

Today's Riddle: Why is a dime smarter than a nickel?

Name: _____ Date: _____

Discover more than one solution

Level: | 4 | 5 | 6 | 7 | 8 |

Fence It In

Directions: Draw lines to create a closed fence. Lines may be drawn vertically or horizontally, but not diagonally. The numbers in the grid indicate the number of sides of the fence that go around that space. Every space with a 2 is bordered by 2 sides of the fence. If a space contains a 3, it is bordered by 3 sides of the fence.

Example:

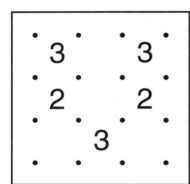

Solution:

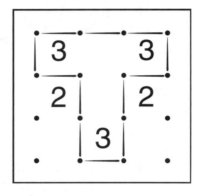

Use the grid and numbers below. Find at least one solution. There are three possible correct answers. Can you find more than one?

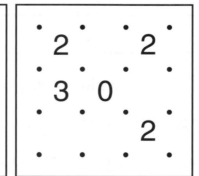

Name: _____ Date: _____

Use math strategy

Level: 4 5 6 7 8

Beware of Triangles

Each player needs a different color of colored pencil.

1. Players take turns drawing a line segment connecting any two dots. The object of the game is to avoid making a triangle with three sides the same color.

2. The player who draws a line that results in three sides of a triangle in the same color loses the game.

3. If a player completes a triangle but all three sides are not the same color, that player receives a point, and the game continues.

4. Use strategy to try to force the other player into making the losing triangle. The player with the most points at the end of the game wins.

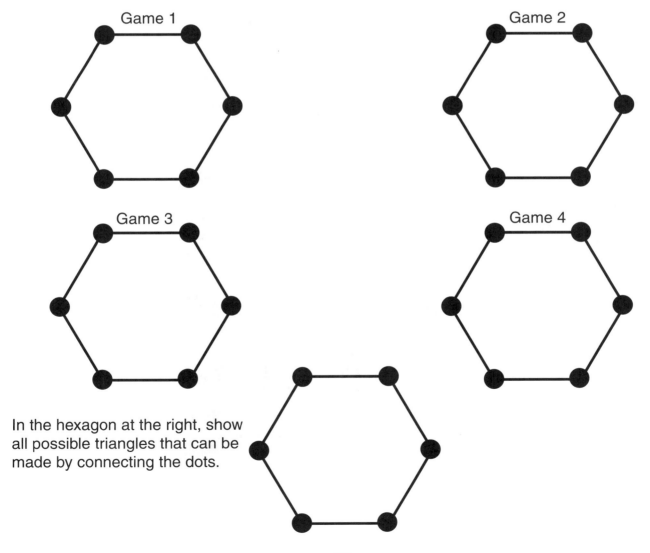

Game 1

Game 2

Game 3

Game 4

In the hexagon at the right, show all possible triangles that can be made by connecting the dots.

Name: _____   Date: _____

Use logic and deductive reasoning to solve a problem   **Level:** 4 | 5 | 6 | 7 | 8

Welcome to Rainbow Apartments

Directions: At the Rainbow Apartments, the trim is painted a different color on each floor. Use the clues below to find out what color the trim is painted on each floor. Write the answers on the lines.

1. The blue trim is on a higher floor than the green trim, but on a lower floor than the one painted yellow.

2. The pink trim is on the floor between the one with yellow trim and the one painted blue.

3. The green trim is on a lower floor than the one with lavender trim.

   What color is the trim on each floor?

RAINBOW APARTMENTS

_____

_____

_____

_____

_____

Name: _____ Date: _____

Use logic and deductive reasoning/Mixed operations   **Level:** | 4 | 5 | 6 | 7 | 8 |

Brain Teasers

Directions: Can you solve these without too much brain strain? **Hint:** It might help to draw pictures as you investigate possible solutions.

A. A hamburger and bun costs $2.10. The hamburger costs $2 more than the bun.
How much does the bun cost? _____

B. Tina is three times as old as her brother Marco. In six years, Tina will be twice as old as Marco.
How old is Tina now? _____
How old is Marco now? _____

C. It takes four carpenters four minutes to nail four sheets of paneling in place.
How long will it take 120 carpenters to nail 120 sheets of paneling in place? _____

D. Ivan made a display of books for the library. He put three books in the top row. There are three more books in each row than in the row above. Ivan's display was eight rows high.
How many books in all did Ivan use? _____

E. Stephanie has twice as many CDs as Trevor. If she gave Trevor two CDs, they would both have the same number.
How many CDs does Stephanie have? _____
How many CDs does Trevor have? _____

F. You need to add up a list of numbers from zero to 100. Rather than adding 1 + 2 + 3 + 4, etc., there is an easier way to do it. Explain how. **Hint:** Think about the numbers at the opposite ends of the list and how they relate to each other. (0 and 100, 99 and 1, etc.)

_____

_____

_____

Name: _____   Date: _____

Use logic and deductive reasoning   **Level:** 4   5   6   7   8

Pick-Up Sticks

Directions:

A. Remove three sticks from the five squares and leave three squares. Show your answer by crossing out the sticks to be removed. **Hint:** Arrange toothpicks in this pattern, and then move them around until you find the answer.

B. Use the six sticks to make four triangles. **Hint:** Toothpicks will help with this one too.

Show your answer here:

Name: _____ Date: _____

Use logic and deductive reasoning

Level: 4 5 6 7 8

Banner Day

Directions: Use the following information to answer the questions below.

- Anna, Barb, and Carrie are each making a banner exactly nine feet long. Each will use three colors of paper: red, blue, and gold.

- Anna selected the blue and gold paper that was the same size.

- Barb chose the longest piece of blue paper.

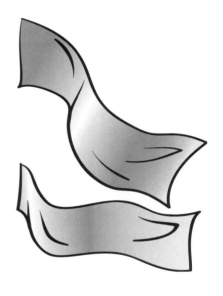

Available Paper for Banners		
Red	Gold	Blue
42"	24"	28"
4'	$2\frac{1}{2}'$	3'
48"	38"	30"

A.   How much of each color did each girl select?

	Red	Gold	Blue
Anna			
Barb			
Carrie			

B.   Todd, Jacob, and Tony created a banner for the Math Fair. Everyone who attended tried to solve it. Can you?

Even up the totals in each streamer by moving one number to another streamer.

Math Fair

2	8	14
4	10	16
6	12	18

Name: _____   Date: _____

Use deductive reasoning/Mixed operations   **Level:** ■■■■■ 5 6 7 8

Master Math Challenges

Directions: Merlin the Mighty Master Math Magician had his pet tarantula send a message on the web calling all minor math magicians to a meeting. When they arrived, he gave them three challenges. If you can solve all three challenges, you too will become a master math magician.

Five master math magicians are writing 98-page magic math books.

- Abby has 36 pages left to write in her magic geometry book.

- Brett has 11 fewer pages to write in his magic fractions book than Tomás has in his magic algebra book.

- Tomás has written 4 fewer pages in his magic algebra book than Abby has in her magic geometry book.

- Mia has written 2 more pages in her magic multiplication book than Brett has in his magic fractions book.

- Luis has written 5 more pages in his magic division book than Abby did in her magic geometry book.

A.   How many pages has each one written?

   Abby _____ Brett _____ Luis _____ Mia _____ Tomás _____

Merlin has three magic beanstalks in his garden. The leaves on all three beanstalks start one foot above the ground. Above that point, there is one leaf every four inches. The three beanstalks in Merlin's garden are four, six, and nine feet tall.

B.   How many leaves are there altogether on Merlin's magic beanstalks? _____

Merlin counted 44 heads and 128 legs in a group of dragons and dragon riders.

C.   How many four-legged dragons were in the group? _____

D.   How many two-legged dragon riders were in the group? _____

Name: _____ Date: _____

Use logic and deductive reasoning   **Level:** | 4 | 5 | 6 | 7 | 8 |

Twins Convention

Directions: Use deductive reasoning and the clues below to find the names of each set of twins and the day of the week they arrived at the Twins Convention. Put an "N" for "No" in the appropriate boxes on the grid as you read the clues and eliminate possibilities. Put a "Y" in the appropriate boxes for "Yes."

	Al	Bob	Cal	Nick	Sam	Mon	Tue	Wed	Thu	Fri
Anna										
Beth										
Dana										
Ellen										
Jill										
Mon										
Tue										
Wed										
Thu										
Fri										

Five sets of twins went to the Twins Convention. Each set arrived on a different day of the week.
1. All sets of twins consist of a boy and girl.
2. Anna and her twin arrived on Monday.
3. Al isn't Anna's twin.
4. Cal and his twin arrived on Wednesday.
5. Sam arrived on Friday, but not with Jill.
6. Nick and Ellen are twins. They arrived the day after Dana and her twin.

The twins are: They arrived on:

A.   Anna and _____   _____

B.   Beth and _____   _____

C.   Dana and _____   _____

D.   Ellen and _____   _____

E.   Jill and _____   _____

Name: _____   Date: _____

Use logic and deductive reasoning

Level: ▮▮▮▮ 5 6 7 8

Party Time

Directions: Four friends worked together to throw an end-of-the-summer party. From the clues given, determine each person's last name, the job each performed, and the color of T-shirt each person wore. Write "N" for "No" or "Y" for "Yes" in the grid. Use a pencil in case you need to erase.

1. The one who made the food wore a red T-shirt and had a first name two letters longer than the one who sent the invitations.

2. The person whose last name was Carlson wore a green T-shirt.

3. Carlos's last name was Juarez, but Rob's wasn't O'Brien.

4. The person whose last name was Edwards decorated for the party and had a first name that was one letter longer than the person who wore the blue T-shirt.

	Juarez	Carlson	Edwards	O'Brien	Red	Blue	Green	Purple	Made food	Invitations	Decorated	Cleaned up
Rob												
Tina												
Maria												
Carlos												
Made food					Y	N	N	N				
Invitations					N							
Decorated					N							
Cleaned up					N							
Red												
Blue												
Green												
Purple												

First Name	Last Name	Job	Color T-shirt
Rob			
Tina			
Maria			
Carlos			

Name: _____ Date: _____

Use deductive reasoning/Algebra/Mixed operations   **Level:** | 4 | 5 | 6 | 7 | 8 |

Brain Benders

Directions: Find the answers. **Hint:** It might help to draw pictures on scrap paper as you investigate possible solutions.

A.   What three consecutive numbers have a sum of 150? _____ _____ _____

B.   Scott and Tyrone play basketball. The sum of their heights is 13 feet, 4 inches. Scott is 2 inches taller than Tyrone. How tall is each player?

   Scott: _____   Tyrone: _____

C.   There are three children in the Heimerdinger family: Harry, Henry, and Hannah. They are 2, 6, and 8 years old. Harry is older than Henry. Henry was born when Hannah was six years old.

   How old is each child? Harry: _____   Henry: _____   Hannah: _____

D.   On a field trip, two school buses drove in front of a school bus and two school buses drove behind a school bus in a single-file line.

   What is the fewest number of school buses that could be driving together on the trip?

   _____

E.   Each school bus held a maximum of 48 passengers.

   Bus 1 was $\frac{2}{3}$ full.

   Bus 2 was $\frac{1}{4}$ empty.

   Bus 3 had 87.5% of the maximum number of passengers.

   How many passengers were on the three buses? _____

F.   Jason's grandfather is four times older than he is. The sum of Jason's age and his grandfather's age is 80.

   How old is Jason? _____

G.   At a farmer's market, a bushel of potatoes cost $10, a 50-pound bag of onions cost $5, and pumpkins were $1 each.

   How many different combinations of vegetables could you buy if you spent $26? _____

Name: _____

Date: _____

Calculate discount and sale price

Level: 4 5 6 7 8

Hattie's Hat Sale

Directions: Help Hattie get ready for her holiday hat sale. Write the sale price of each hat on the corresponding starburst. Use a calculator. Round prices to the nearest cent.

DISCOUNT	TYPE OF HAT	ORIGINAL PRICE	SALE PRICE
A. 15 %		$ 19.95	A. SALE PRICE!
B. 27 %		$ 129.47	B. SALE PRICE!
C. 75 %		$537.26	C. SALE PRICE!
D. 12 %		$ 24.89	D. SALE PRICE!
E. 31 %		$ 41.02	E. SALE PRICE!
F. 11 %		$ 11.11	F. SALE PRICE!
G. 9 %	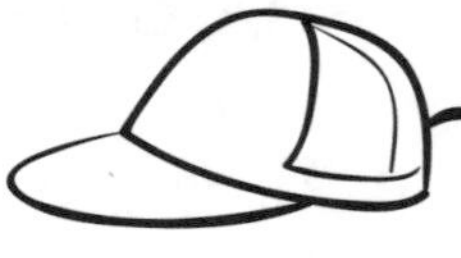	$ 9.99	G. SALE PRICE!
H. 14 %		$ 127.51	H. SALE PRICE!
I. 16 %		$ 16.82	I. SALE PRICE!
J. 42 %		$ 31.86	J. SALE PRICE!

Name: _____ Date: _____

Calculate unit cost/Compare costs

Level: 4 5 6 7 8

Comparing Costs

Directions: Which costs less per item? Circle the lower price in each group.

A.   Corn: 4 cans for $1.39 or 6 cans for $1.92

B.   Juice: 3 cans for $0.98 or 4 cans for $1.37

C.   Cashews: 2 pounds for $4.59 or 6 pounds for $13.76

D.   Onions: 2 pounds for $0.69 or 5 pounds for $1.61

E.   Apples: 10 for $1.64 or 12 for $2.01

F.   Pens: 5 for $1.25 or 3 for $0.69

G.   Folders: 6 for $2.67 or 4 for $1.79

H.   Soda: 6 16-ounce bottles for $1.99 or 12 8-ounce cans for $1.59

I.   Potatoes: 10 pounds for $2.98 or 50 pounds for $13.54

J.   Cheese: 1 pound for $4.17 or 10 pounds for $41.77

K.   Eggs: 1 dozen for $0.89 or 18 for $1.29

L.   Milk: 1 gallon for $2.98 or 1 quart for $1.29

M.   Buns: 12 for $3.47 or 8 for $2.54

N.   Hot dogs: 2 pounds for $2.12 or 5 pounds for $5.75

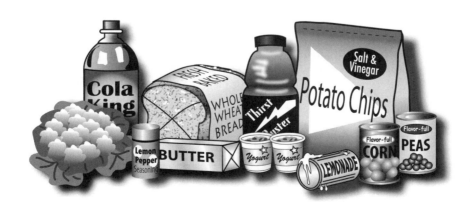

Name: _____ Date: _____

Calculate wages/overtime/vacation pay

Level: 4 5 6 7 8

Help Wanted

At the XYZ Factory, workers are paid by the hour. They receive time and a half for all hours worked over 40 in a week.

Directions: Calculate the weekly pay for these workers:

Name	Hourly Rate	Hours Worked	Gross Pay
Abby	$10.75	42	_____
Ben	$12.50	48	_____
Carlos	$15.15	45	_____
Dana	$11.90	40.5	_____
Eduardo	$13.48	44.5	_____

A.   Greg earns $14.50 per hour. He worked exactly the same number of hours each week for the past four weeks. His total pay, including overtime, for that period was $2,668.

How many hours per week did he work? _____

Vacation pay is based on gross pay for the previous year. One week of vacation is paid at 2% of last year's gross pay.

B.   Dana earned $25,644 last year. How much will she receive for one week of vacation?

_____

C.   Carlos earned $33,784 last year. He receives three weeks of vacation. What will his total vacation pay be this year?

_____

Workers at the XYZ Factory were given two options.
  1) They could work four twelve-hour days one week and three twelve-hour days the next week
                                          or
  2) They could work five nine-hour days per week.

D.   Which option would you select? _____

E.   Why? _____

_____

_____

Name: _____ Date: _____

Compare prices

Level: 4 5 6 7 8

Then and Now

Everything was cheaper in the good old days, right? Not necessarily.

Microwave ovens were first introduced in Mansfield, Ohio, by the Tappan Company on October 25, 1955. The price tag: $1,200.

A.   Check the prices of microwaves at stores, in newspaper ads, or online. Fill in the information for three different models. Compare the prices then and now.

Brand name	Size	Price	Difference between now and 1955
_____	_____	_____	_____
_____	_____	_____	_____
_____	_____	_____	_____

In 1945, Gimbels Department Store in New York City was the first to sell commercially-made ballpoint pens. The pens sold for $12.50 each.

B.   Check the price of a disposable ballpoint pen today. _____

How much less does a ballpoint pen cost today than it did in 1945? _____

It cost $10 to see the first talking picture, "Don Juan," starring John Barrymore. The black and white movie was first shown at New York's Warner Theater on August 6, 1926.

C.   How much more (or less) does a ticket to a movie cost today where you live than in 1926? _____

Imagine paying $850 for a new car! That's what it cost to buy the new Model T introduced by Henry Ford on October 1, 1908.

D.   Check the price on three new Ford vehicles, like a car, a van, and a pick-up. Look for the lowest prices you can find (stripped-down models, no extras.) Compare the prices then and now.

Type of vehicle	Price	Difference between 1908 and now
_____	_____	_____
_____	_____	_____
_____	_____	_____

Name: _____ Date: _____

Show elapsed time

Level: 4 5 6 7 8

Just Passing Time

Directions: Draw the hands on the second clock in each pair to show the amount of time that has passed.

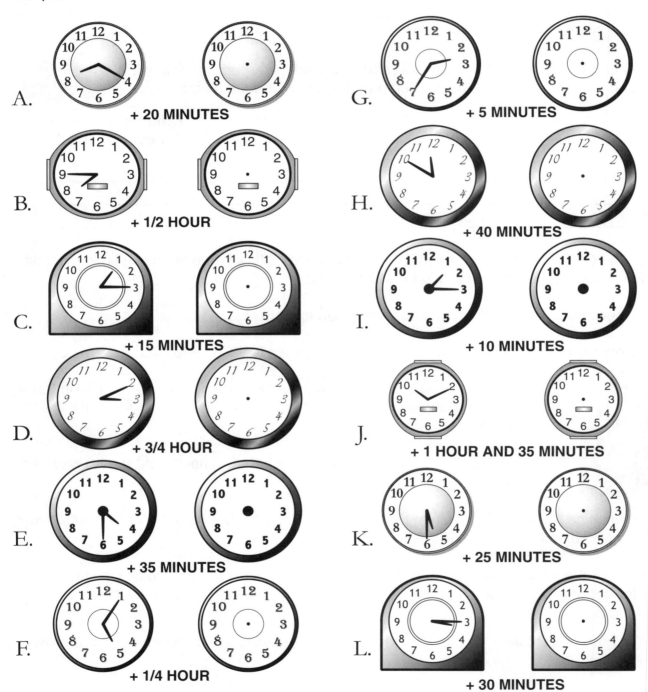

A. **+ 20 MINUTES**

B. **+ 1/2 HOUR**

C. **+ 15 MINUTES**

D. **+ 3/4 HOUR**

E. **+ 35 MINUTES**

F. **+ 1/4 HOUR**

G. **+ 5 MINUTES**

H. **+ 40 MINUTES**

I. **+ 10 MINUTES**

J. **+ 1 HOUR AND 35 MINUTES**

K. **+ 25 MINUTES**

L. **+ 30 MINUTES**

Name: _____ Date: _____

Calculate elapsed time

Level: 4   5   6   7   8

Rock Around the Clock

Directions: Calculate the amount of elapsed time (E.T.) between the first and second clocks in each group. Don't forget to check for A.M. and P.M. on each clock.

8:20 A.M.

12:05 P.M.

A. E.T.: _____ hours, _____ minutes

6:45 A.M.

11:20 A.M.

B. E.T.: _____ hours, _____ minutes

1:15 P.M.

11:20 P.M.

C. E.T.: _____ hours, _____ minutes

3:10 A.M.

2:15 P.M.

D. E.T.: _____ hours, _____ minutes

4:30 A.M.

12:05 P.M.

E. E.T.: _____ hours, _____ minutes

5:05 A.M.

10:00 A.M.

F. E.T.: _____ hours, _____ minutes

2:35 P.M.

9:25 P.M.

G. E.T.: _____ hours, _____ minutes

11:50 A.M.

11:55 P.M.

H. E.T.: _____ hours, _____ minutes

1:15 A.M.

11:40 P.M.

I. E.T.: _____ hours, _____ minutes

10:10 P.M.

6:20 A.M.

J. E.T.: _____ hours, _____ minutes

5:30 P.M.

11:40 A.M.

K. E.T.: _____ hours, _____ minutes

3:15 P.M.

3:45 A.M.

L. E.T.: _____ hours, _____ minutes

Name: _____ Date: _____

Sequencing

Level: 4 5 6 7 8

Step by Step

Directions: Look at the diagrams below. Each diagram represents a step in the shading of the final picture. Number the diagrams to show the order in which the squares were shaded.

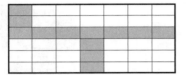

A. _____

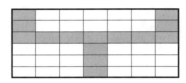

B. _____

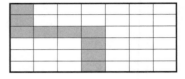

C. _____

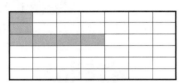

D. _____

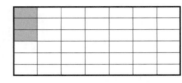

E. _____

F. _____

G. Write the steps, in order, needed to calculate the cost of new carpeting for a room.

_____

_____

_____

_____

_____

_____

_____

_____

H. Draw in the steps needed to divide a pizza into eight equal pieces.

 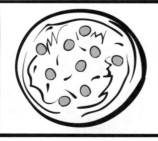  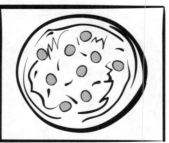

Today's Riddle: How many bushels of dirt can you take from a hole four feet deep and four feet wide?

Name: _____ Date: _____

Extend a pattern/Create a chart   **Level:** | 4 | 5 | 6 | 7 | 8 |

Sheila Sees Seashells by the Seashore

Sheila arranged seashells in triangular shapes.

1.

2.

3.

A. How many seashells are on each side of the first triangle? _____
B. How many seashells are on each side of the second triangle? _____
C. How many seashells are on each side of the third triangle? _____
D. How many seashells are in the first triangle? _____
E. How many seashells are in the second triangle? _____
F. How many seashells are in the third triangle? _____
G. If she continues the pattern, how many seashells will Sheila use on each side of the next triangle? _____
H. Use your answers to complete the chart for six triangles following the same pattern.

Triangle	1	2	3	4	5	6
Number of shells on each side						
Total number of shells						

Super Challenge: If Sheila extended this pattern, how many seashells would be on each side of the 20th triangle? _____

How many seashells would be in the 20th triangle? _____

Hint: Look for a repeating pattern in your chart.

Name: _____   Date: _____

Continue the patterns   **Level:** ▨▨▨ 5 6 7 8

Pascal's Triangle

Directions: Follow the pattern to complete the next six rows in Pascal's* Triangle.

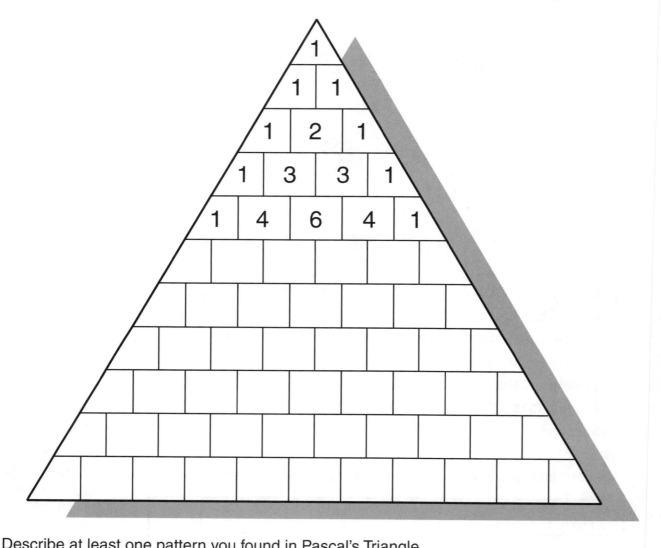

Describe at least one pattern you found in Pascal's Triangle.

_____

_____

_____

_____

*   Blaise Pascal was a French scientist, philosopher, and mathematical prodigy. His contributions to mathematics
    include: the formulation of probability theory, the development of differential calculus, as well as Pascal's Law
    and Pascal's Triangle.

Name: _____ Date: _____

Exploring arithmetic sequences   **Level:** ▮▮▮▮▮▮ 7 ▮ 8 ▮

A Non-Stop Difference

In the **arithmetic sequence** { 5, 11, 17, 23, 29, . . . } each number is obtained from the previous number by adding the same number, in this case 6, which is called the **common difference**.

Directions: Write the next five terms and the common difference for each of the following arithmetic sequences.

A.   3, 15, 27, 39, 51, ____, ____, ____, ____, ____   Common difference = ____

B.   37, 115, 193, 271, ____, ____, ____, ____, ____   Common difference = ____

C.   81, 64, 47, 30, ____, ____, ____, ____, ____   Common difference = ____

For some sequences, it is difficult to quickly determine the pattern of differences. For example, if you look at this sequence { 2, 5, 13, 26, 44, . . . }, it is not a simple matter to immediately detect the pattern of differences between the numbers. So we can use an approach called **finite differences** to discover the underlying pattern. Here's a picture of how it works:

```
   2        5        13       26       44      (57)     (85)
       3        8        13       18     (23)     (28)
          5        5        5        5        5
```

We call this an **algebraic sequence** since each difference is an increasing multiple of five added to the number 3. Notice that the differences that are in the second row in the figure above have the following form: **3** = 3 + 0 * 5, **8** = 3 + 1 * 5, **13** = 3 + 2 * 5, etc. Hence, if we let n stand for which difference we are adding, then the nth difference = 3 + $(n - 1)$ * 5. The method used above is called the **method of finite differences**. Sometimes there are more than two levels, but the process always continues until we reach a line of constants, so that we can work our way backwards to the next number in the original sequence.

Directions: Find the next four numbers for each sequence below:

D.   1, 5, 12, 22, 35, ____, ____, ____, ____

E.   -7, -2, 8, 23, 43, ____, ____, ____, ____

F.   1, 5, 14, 30, 55, ____, ____, ____, ____   [Hint: You will need 3 rows.]

Name: _____ Date: _____

Exploring geometric sequences   **Level:** ▮▮▮▮▮▮▮ 7   8 ▮

A Non-Stop Product

In a **geometric sequence**, each number is obtained by multiplying the previous number by a common ratio. Can you find the common multiplier in the following sequence? { 3, 15, 75, 375, . . . } Clearly, the next number in the sequence is 1875, since the common ratio is the number five.

Directions: Find the common ratio and the next three numbers for each geometric sequence below:

A.   1, 7, 49, 343, _____, _____, _____   Common ratio = _____

B.   4, -12, 36, -108, _____, _____, _____   Common ratio = _____

The second geometric sequence above is called an **alternating sequence** because it changes its sign, alternating between positive and negative, since the common multiplier is a negative number. The common ratio may also be a fraction with an absolute value less than one.

Directions: Repeat the exercise above for the following geometric sequences:

C.   243, 81, 27, 9, _____, _____, _____   Common ratio = _____

D.   -32, 8, -2, $\frac{1}{2}$, _____, _____, _____   Common ratio = _____

The common ratio may also be any real number greater than one in absolute value.

Directions: Once again, find the next three terms and the common ratio for the following geometric sequences:

E. $\frac{81}{4}$, 27, 36, 48, _____, _____, _____   Common ratio = _____

F.   -4, 6, -9, $\frac{27}{2}$, _____, _____, _____   Common ratio = _____

Directions: Determine whether or not each sequence below is arithmetic, geometric, or algebraic, and then find the next four terms for each of them.

Type of sequence

G.   2, 6, 12, 20, 30, _____, _____, _____, _____   _____

H. $\frac{3}{2}$, -1, $\frac{2}{3}$, $\frac{4}{-9}$, $\frac{8}{27}$, _____, _____, _____, _____   _____

I.   -45, -21, 3, 27, 51, _____, _____, _____, _____   _____

J.   -4, $4\sqrt{3}$, -12, $12\sqrt{3}$, -36, _____, _____, _____, _____   _____

Name: _____   Date: _____

Solve equations using mixed operations   **Level:** | 4 | 5 | 6 | 7 | 8 |

Happily Ever After

Directions: Fill in the blanks with numbers of your choosing, and then solve the equations.

Long ago a frog prince lived in a far-off land, _____ miles from the palace. He decided to visit the palace, but could only hop _____ miles per day. It took him _____ days to reach the palace.

Finally he arrived at _____ P.M. on Friday, the 13th. He waited for 12 hours and 25 minutes. By the time he met the king, it was _____ A.M.

When he entered the throne room, he saw _____ rows of guards. There were _____ guards in each row. Wow! That made a total of _____ guards protecting the king.

"Why all the guards?" he wondered. Then he saw the king's fabulous crown. There were _____ emeralds, _____ rubies, and _____ diamonds in the crown. Each emerald was worth $_____. He knew a ruby that size cost $_____. And diamonds! Surely ones that large cost $_____ each. The total cost of the jewels in the crown came to $_____. No wonder there were so many guards.

"Welcome, Frog Prince," said the king. "I supposed you've come to marry the princess, turn into a prince, and live happily ever after."

"If it pleases your majesty, yes," replied the Frog Prince.

"Hmpff!" said the king. "Same old thing. Oh, well, you know the drill. Before you can marry the princess, you must complete three tasks. However, we have a special today. You only need to complete two tasks."

"Your first task is to divide my 319 gold nuggets into piles with the same number in each pile."

"That's easy," replied the Frog Prince as he made _____ piles with _____ gold nuggets in each pile.

"Very good," said the king. "Your second task is to arrange the numbers from 16 to 24 in three columns and three rows so that every column, row, and diagonal adds up to 60. I'll even give you a hint," said the king. "The middle number is 20."

Show how the frog completed the final task.

	20	

If you helped the Frog Prince complete both tasks correctly, you're invited to the wedding.

Name: _____ Date: _____

Solve equations for *x*

Level: 3 4   5   6   7   8

Tic-Tac-Go

1. Players take turns solving equations. If the answer is correct, the player puts an "X" or an "O" in that space.

2. The first player to get three "X's" or "O's" in a row is the winner.

A.

$x + 17 = 21$	$43 + x = 82$	$x + 8 - 2 = 9$
$3 + x + 4 = 14$	$x - 6 + 1 = 2$	$7 - x + 3 = 10$
$5 + x + 2 = 9$	$8 - 3 + x = 11$	$x - 3 - 2 = 7$

B.

$4 + x + 2 = 14$	$7 - x = 3$	$8 + x = 15$
$x + 3 - 6 = 9$	$7 + x - 4 = 4$	$13 - x + 5 = 13$
$6 + x + 4 = 20$	$x + 7 = 7 + 3$	$9 - 3 = x - 4$

C.

$3x = 9$	$7x = 42$	$4x = 48$
$5x = 25$	$8x = 56$	$6x = 66$
$10x = 120$	$2x = 444$	$9x = 63$

D.

$24 \div x = 6$	$x \div 9 = 9$	$42 \div x = 6$
$x \div 9 = 6$	$100 \div x = 10$	$x \div 11 = 8$
$50 \div x = 2$	$x \div 8 = 9$	$75 \div x = 3$

Name: _____ Date: _____

Write algebraic expressions

Level: 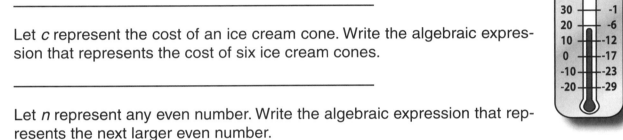 4 5 6 7 8

Let *t* Represent Temperature

Directions: Write an algebraic expression for each statement. Use the variables given.

Example: Let *c* represent the cost of a pizza. Write the algebraic expression that represents the cost of three pizzas. *c* * 3 or 3*c*

A. Let *t* represent the temperature at 6 A.M. Write the algebraic expression that represents the temperature after it rises 21 degrees.

_____

B. Let *c* represent the cost of an ice cream cone. Write the algebraic expression that represents the cost of six ice cream cones.

_____

C. Let *n* represent any even number. Write the algebraic expression that represents the next larger even number.

_____

D. Let *w* represent any whole number. Write the algebraic expressions that represent the next three whole numbers.

_____

E. Let *s* represent the speed of a car in miles per hour. Write the algebraic expression that represents a decrease in speed of 20 mph.

_____

F. Let *h* represent the height of a hot air balloon. Write the algebraic expression that represents a 25% increase in height.

_____

G. Let *s* represent the number of seconds in one day. Write the algebraic expression that represents the number of seconds in one week.

_____

H. Let *m* represent the price of a meal. Write the algebraic expression that represents a 15% tip.

_____

Name: _____ Date: _____

Solve addition and subtraction equations with variables **Level:** | 5 | 6 | 7 | 8 |

X Marks the Spot

Each player needs a different colored pencil and one die.

Directions:

1. Both players roll one die. The player with the higher number selects any equation to solve. If correct, the player colors in that space. Players check each other's answers.

2. If both players roll the same number, both roll again.

3. Only the player with the higher number takes a turn each round.

4. The player with the most spaces colored is the winner.

$a + 14 = 21$	$d - 5 = 72$
$i - 0 = 935$	$7 + p = 71$
$c + 1 = 101$	$14 - y = 9$
$71 - m = 48$	$33 + j = 31$
$68 - o = 45$	$36 - s = 21$
$e + 15 = 45$	$t + 75 = 116$
$k + 11 = 365$	$4 + b = 19$
$p + 21 = 47$	$17 - r = 1$
$z - 3 = 76$	$n + 22 = 622$
$x + 7 = 11$	$h + 32 = 104$
$13 - w = 9$	$11 - f = 4$
$q + 50 = 155$	$l - 19 = 11$
$x - 10 = 47$	$100 - r = 4$
$5 - y = 3$	$u - 2 = 34$
$g - 19 = 91$	$8 + v = 58$
$3 + z = 41$	$16 - m = 3$

Name: _____ Date: _____

Write and solve equations

Level: 4 5 6 7 8

World Records

Directions: Write the equation and circle the solution for each world record story. Round answers to the nearest tenth.

Pizza lovers in Havana, Florida, created a pizza covering 10,057 square feet in 1991, but it didn't set the record. An even larger one had been made the year before in Norwood, South Africa. That monster pizza measured 122.66 feet in diameter.

A. What was the area of this monster pizza? _____

Equation: _____

B. How much larger was it than the one made in Florida? _____

Equation: _____

A high temperature of 134° F was recorded in Death Valley, California, on July 10, 1913. A record low of -79.8° was set at Prospect Creek, Alaska, on June 23, 1971.

C. How much difference was there between these two temperatures? _____

Equation: _____

A record-breaking apple pie contained over 600 bushels of apples and weighed 30,115 pounds. Baked in a 40- by 23-foot dish, this super pie was made in England.

D. What was the area of the dish? _____

Equation: _____

E. What was the perimeter of the dish? _____

Equation: _____

In 1976, Kathy Wafler peeled a 20-ounce apple in one long, unbroken peel that was 172 feet, 4 inches long.

F. How long was the peeling in inches? _____

Equation: _____

G. How long was it in yards? _____

Equation: _____

Did You Know? Taco Tico of Nebraska, Inc., set a record in 1991 for the world's largest burrito: 1,597 feet, 9 inches long. Made from 2,557 tortillas, this colossal burrito contained 607 pounds of refried beans and 75.75 pounds of shredded cheese!

Name: _____   Date: _____

Solve multiplication equations with one variable   **Level:** 4 5 6 7 8

Alien Invasion

Each player needs a die and a different colored pencil.

Directions:

1. Each player rolls one die. The player with the higher number selects any UFO and solves the equation. If correct, that player colors in that UFO. Players check each other's answers.

2. If both players roll the same number, both roll again.

3. Only the player with the higher number takes a turn each round.

4. The player with the most UFOs colored wins.

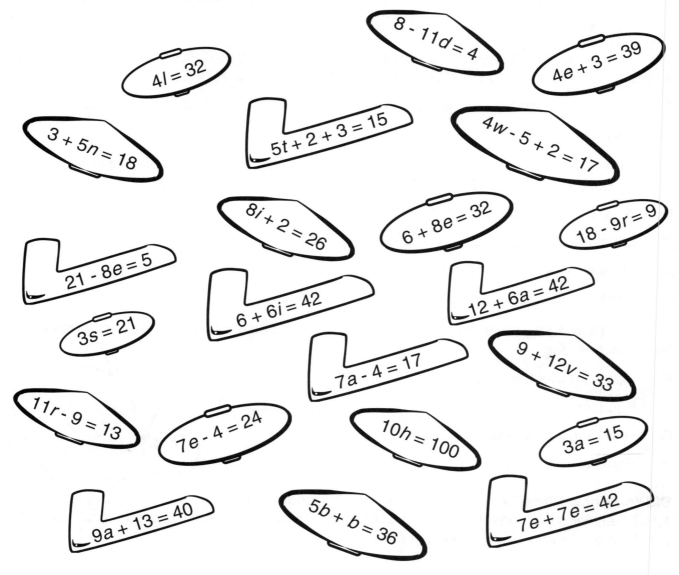

$4l = 32$

$8 - 11d = 4$

$4e + 3 = 39$

$3 + 5n = 18$

$5t + 2 + 3 = 15$

$4w - 5 + 2 = 17$

$8i + 2 = 26$

$6 + 8e = 32$

$18 - 9r = 9$

$21 - 8e = 5$

$6 + 6i = 42$

$12 + 6a = 42$

$3s = 21$

$7a - 4 = 17$

$9 + 12v = 33$

$11r - 9 = 13$

$7e - 4 = 24$

$10h = 100$

$3a = 15$

$9a + 13 = 40$

$5b + b = 36$

$7e + 7e = 42$

Name: _____ Date: _____

Solve division equations with one variable

Level: 5 6 7 8

Reach for the Stars

You will need four dice, colored pencils, and paper. Each player needs a different colored pencil.

Directions:

1. Players decide how many dice to roll on each turn: one, two, three, or four. The total number on the dice represents the number of the star. Each player must solve the equation on the star with the corresponding number. If correct, the player colors in that star.

2. Players check each other's answers. If a star has already been colored, that player skips a turn. The player with the most stars colored is the winner.

1. $\dfrac{a}{2} = 8$

2. $\dfrac{b}{7} = 1$

3. $\dfrac{12}{c} = 3$

4. $\dfrac{11}{d} = 2$

9. $\dfrac{i}{5} = 5$

5. $\dfrac{e}{9} = \dfrac{1}{3}$

6. $\dfrac{8}{f} = 2$

7. $\dfrac{6}{g} = \dfrac{3}{5}$

8. $\dfrac{7}{h} = 3$

12. $\dfrac{l}{5} = 2$

13. $\dfrac{3}{k} = 1$

14. $\dfrac{j}{4} = 4$

11. $\dfrac{10}{n} = 100$

10. $\dfrac{q}{8} = 7$

16. $\dfrac{4}{s} = \dfrac{1}{4}$

17. $\dfrac{p}{10} = 3$

18. $\dfrac{7}{r} = \dfrac{1}{7}$

19. $\dfrac{u}{5} = 25$

15. $\dfrac{2}{m} = 12$

20. $\dfrac{3}{x} = \dfrac{1}{3}$

21. $\dfrac{9}{w} = 3$

22. $\dfrac{y}{19} = 2$

23. $\dfrac{v}{6} = 6$

24. $\dfrac{11}{t} = 11$

Name: _____ Date: _____

Identify congruent figures

Level: 4 5 6 7 8

Every Which Way

Congruent figures are the same size and shape, even if they are turned in different directions.

These two figures are congruent: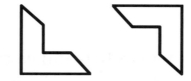

Directions: Circle the hat in each row that is congruent to the first one.

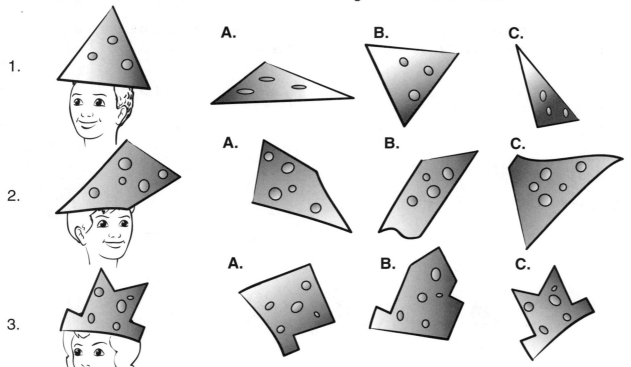

1. A. B. C.

2. A. B. C.

3. A. B. C.

Directions: Draw hats that are congruent to the ones shown.

4.

5.

Name: _____ Date: _____

Rotate geometric figures

Level: 4 5 6 7 8

Before the Wheel

Before the wheel was invented, cave people may have experimented with other shapes. If they tried to use a triangle, it would look like this as the caveman pushed his cart.

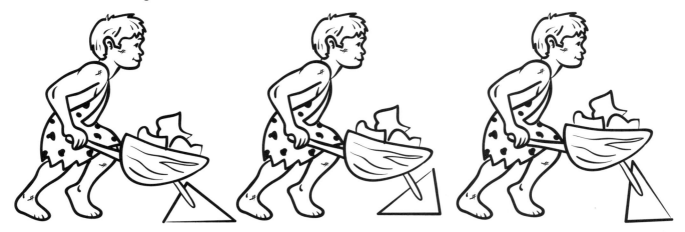

Directions: Finish the pictures in each row. Draw the shape in each panel to show how it would look as the caveman pushed his cart.

Name: _____   Date: _____

Three-dimensional thinking

Level: | | 4 | 5 | 6 | 7 | 8 |

Cube It

This 4″ x 4″ cube was painted blue, then cut into one-inch cubes.

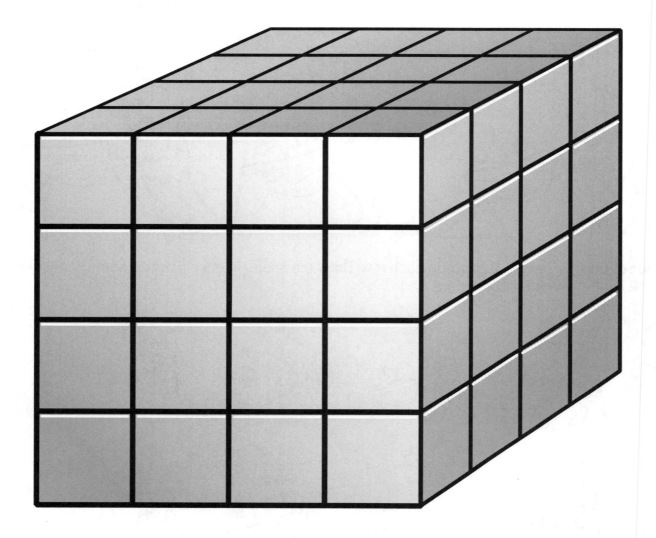

A.   How many 1″ cubes are there? _____

B.   Have many 1″ cubes have no paint on them? _____

C.   How many of the 1″ cubes are painted on one side only? _____

D.   How many of the 1″ cubes are painted on only two sides? _____

E.   How many of the 1″ cubes are painted on three sides? _____

Name: _____   Date: _____

Calculate perimeters of irregular shapes   **Level:** 4 5 6 7 8

Surround It

Perimeter is the distance around an object.

Example: The perimeter of this rectangle is 2 + 6 + 6 + 2 = 16 units.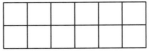

Directions: Write the perimeter of each shape.

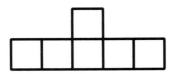

A. _____ units

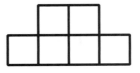

B. _____ units

C. _____ units

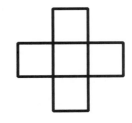

D. _____ units

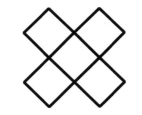

E. _____ units

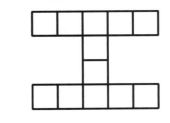

F. _____ units

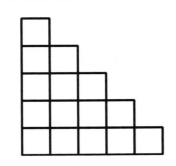

G. _____ units

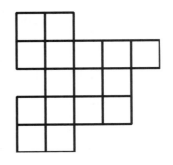

H. _____ units

I.   Which four figures have the same perimeter? _____

Name: _____   Date: _____

Find area   Level: 4 5 6 7 8

Directions: Use the following formulas to find the areas of the shapes below. Write the area in square inches.

Area of a rectangle = (**l** x **w**): **length** times **width**.

Area of a triangle = ($\frac{1}{2}$)**b** x **h** : ($\frac{1}{2}$)**base** times **height**.

A.   Area = _____   B.   Area = _____

l = 8″
w = 5″ |← 8" →| b = 8″
            [rectangle 5"]   h = 9″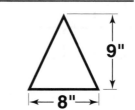

Look closely at the figures below, and then answer the questions.

Figure C   **Figure D**   **Figure E**

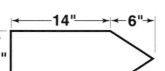   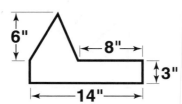

Figure F   **Figure G**

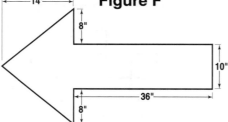   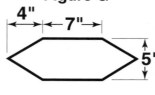

C.   Figure C is actually two rectangles. Find the area of each rectangle, and add the two to-
      gether to find the total area of the figure.   Area = _____

D.   What two shapes make up Figure D? _____

      How can you find the area of this shape? _____

      _____   Area = _____

E.   What two shapes make up Figure E? _____

      Area = _____

F.   What is the area of Figure F?   Area: _____

G.   What is the area of Figure G?   Area: _____

Name: _____   Date: _____

Calculate perimeter/Area/Price

Level: 4 5 6 7 8

Waldo's Wonderful World of Wallpaper

Directions: Use the information given to find the answers to the questions below.

Jason wants to buy enough wallpaper border to go completely around his bedroom. The room is 12′ 9″ wide and 14′ 4″ long. Wallpaper border comes in 15-foot rolls.

A.   What is the perimeter of Jason's room? _____

B.   How many 15-foot rolls of wallpaper border will Jason need? Round your answer up to the nearest full roll.

_____

C.   What is the area of Jason's room? (Note: 144 square inches = 1 square foot)

_____

D.   How many square yards of carpeting would he need? (Note: 1 square yard = 9 square feet.)

_____

Sara is selecting wallpaper border for the dining room. The room is 10′ 6″ wide and 11′ 4″ long.

E.   What is the perimeter of the dining room? _____

F.   How many 15-foot rolls of wallpaper border will she need? Round your answer up to the nearest full roll.

_____

G.   If each roll costs $8.97, how much will it cost for the wallpaper border in the dining room?

_____

Measure a room in your house or school.

H.   How long is it?   _____

I.   How wide is it?   _____

J.   What is the perimeter of the room?   _____

K.   How many 15-foot rolls of wallpaper border would you need for that room?   _____

L.   What is the area of the room?   _____

M.   How many square yards of carpeting would you need for that room?   _____

Name: _____   Date: _____

Differentiate between types of angles

Level: | 5 | 6 | 7 | 8 |

Time for Angles

An **acute angle** is greater than 0°and less than 90°.

A **right angle** is exactly 90°.

An **obtuse angle** is greater than 90° and less than 180°.

Directions: Fill in the time by drawing the hands on each clock. Below each clock, write the type of inside angle formed by the hands of the clock. The first one has been done for you.

A. 1:15

Angle: ___acute___

B. 12:35

Angle: _____

C. 3:00

Angle: _____

D. 3:40

Angle: _____

E. 5:00

Angle: _____

F. 12:10

Angle: _____

G. 6:20

Angle: _____

H. 7:30

Angle: _____

I. 3:30

Angle: _____

Name: _____ Date: _____

Calculate angles

Level: 4 5 6 7 8

Always 180°

Directions: Use the following information to complete the exercise.

Every triangle contains three angles.

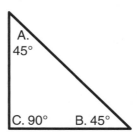

A.   Add angles A, B, and C. _____

The sum of the three angles of a triangle is always 180°, no matter the size or shape of the triangle.

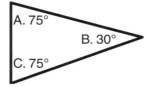

B.   If you know two of the angles, how can you find the third angle? _____

_____

Find the number of degrees in the third angle of each triangle.

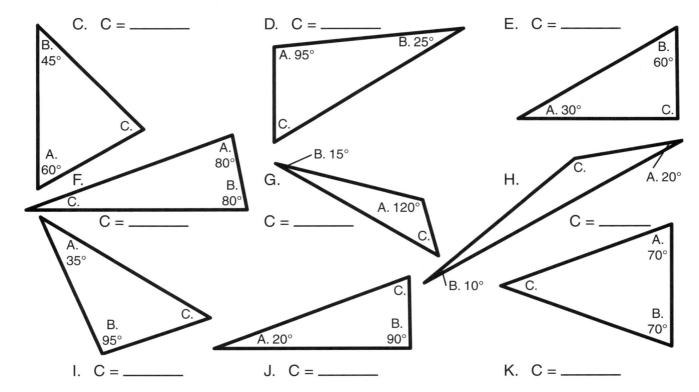

Name: _____   Date: _____

Calculate radius, diameter, and circumference   **Level:** ▌ 5   6   7   8 ▐

Spinning Circles

The **diameter** of a circle is a line segment that passes through the center of a circle and has both end points on the circle. The **radius** of a circle is half of its diameter.

A.   The diameter of a circle is 9 inches. What is its radius? _____

Circumference is the distance around a circle. To find the circumference of any circle, multiply the diameter times 3.14. The number 3.14 is called **pi** and is represented by this Greek symbol, π.

Directions: Find the circumference of each circle. Round to the nearest tenth.

B.   diameter = 4 inches
       circumference = _____

C.   diameter = 3 yards
       circumference = _____

D.   diameter = 6 inches
       circumference = _____

E.   diameter = $3\frac{1}{2}$ feet
       circumference = _____

F.   diameter = 10 miles
       circumference = _____

G.   diameter = 14 inches
       circumference = _____

H.   diameter = 8 feet
       circumference = _____

I.   diameter = 13 miles
       circumference = _____

Fill in the missing numbers.

J.   radius = 1.7 feet

       diameter = _____

       circumference = _____

K.   radius = _____

       diameter = 11 inches

       circumference = _____

L.   radius _____

       diameter = 12 miles

       circumference _____

M.   radius = 2.5 miles

       diameter = _____

       circumference = _____

Name: _____ Date: _____

Calculate radius, diameter, and circumference   **Level:** | 4 | 5 | 6 | 7 | 8 |

Around and Around

$$C = \pi \times d \ \text{ or } \ C = \pi \times 2r$$

C = circumference   **d** = diameter   **r** = radius $\pi = 3.14$

Directions: Round answers to the nearest tenth.

On September 3, 1970, a 1.67-pound hailstone fell in Coffeyville, Texas. The diameter of this huge hailstone was 7.5 inches!

A.   What was its circumference? _____

Earth's moon has an average diameter of 2,159.3 miles.

B.   What is its average circumference? _____

C.   What is its average radius? _____

The first Ferris wheel, named after its constructor George Ferris, was erected in 1893 at the Chicago World's Fair. It had a diameter of 250 feet and carried 36 cars, each capable of holding 60 people.

D.   What was its circumference? _____

E.   How many people could ride at one time? _____

F.   How far, in miles, would one car on the Ferris wheel travel in 10 revolutions? _____

A Ferris wheel erected in Yokohama, Japan, has a diameter of 328 feet.

G.   What is its circumference? _____

H.   What is the difference in circumference between the Ferris wheel in Japan and the one constructed in 1893? _____

In June 1985, a woman in Fresno, California, set a world record for blowing a bubble-gum bubble with a radius of 11 inches.

I.   What was the circumference of the bubble? _____

A clock in Japan has a face 101 feet in diameter. The minute hand is 41 feet long.

J.   How much shorter is the minute hand than the radius of the clock? _____

K.   What is the circumference of this clock? _____

Name: _____   Date: _____

Review properties of lines

Level:  5   6   7   8

What's My Line?

Review

Line: A set of points that extends without end in opposite directions.   A B C

Line segment: Part of a line with two endpoints.   M   N

Ray: A part of a line with one endpoint.   G   H

Intersecting lines: Lines that cross each other.

Parallel lines: Lines on the same plane that never intersect.

Perpendicular lines: Two lines that form a right angle.

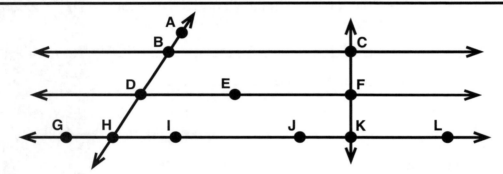

Directions: Use the diagram above to answer the following questions. Use the symbols for lines, line segments, and rays in your answers.

A.   Give an example of a line segment from the diagram. _____

B.   Give an example of a line from the diagram. _____

C.   Give an example of a ray from the diagram. _____

For each pair, write intersecting, parallel, or perpendicular.

D. $\overleftrightarrow{BH}$ and $\overleftrightarrow{GI}$ _____

E. $\overleftrightarrow{CK}$ and $\overleftrightarrow{JL}$ _____

F. $\overleftrightarrow{GI}$ and $\overleftrightarrow{DF}$ _____

G. $\overleftrightarrow{BC}$ and $\overleftrightarrow{BH}$ _____

Name: _____   Date: _____

Compare types of triangles   **Level:** [ ] [5] [6] [7] [8]

Triangle Tango

A **right triangle** has one 90° angle. An **acute triangle** has all angles less than 90°. An **obtuse triangle** has one angle greater than 90° and less than 180°.

An **equilateral triangle** has all sides and angles congruent.

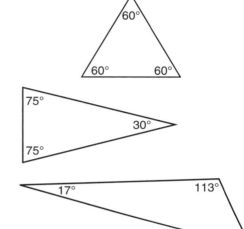

An **isosceles triangle** has two congruent angles and two congruent sides.

A **scalene triangle** has no congruent sides or congruent angles.

A.   Can an equilateral triangle ever be a right triangle? _____

     Why or why not? _____

_____

B.   Can a right triangle ever be a scalene triangle? _____

     Use a drawing to show your answer.

C.   Use a protractor. Draw an example of an obtuse triangle that is also a scalene triangle. Label the three angles and the number of degrees of each angle.

D.   Use a protractor. Draw an acute triangle that is also an equilateral triangle. Label the three angles and the number of degrees of each angle.

Name: _____   Date: _____

Explore space figures   **Level:** 5 6 7 8

These Space Figures Aren't From Mars

A space figure has three dimensions: length, width, and height.

A.   Is a circle a space figure? _____

B.   Is a rectangular prism a space figure? _____

C.   Is a cone a space figure? _____

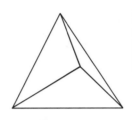 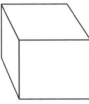   

Tetrahedron   Cube   Octahedron   Dodecahedron   Icosahedron

Faces are the flat surfaces that form a space figure.

D.   Which three space figures shown have triangular faces? _____

_____

E.   Which space figure shown has square faces? _____

F.   Which space figure shown has faces in the shape of a pentagon? _____

G.   How many faces does a cube have? _____

H.   How many faces does a tetrahedron have? _____

I.   Give two examples of items that are cubes. _____

An edge is the intersection of two faces of a space figure.

J.   How many edges does a cube have? _____

K.   How many edges does a tetrahedron have? _____

L.   How many edges does a dodecahedron have? _____

The points where edges meet on a space figure are called vertices. (singular = vertex)

M.   How many vertices does a cube have? _____

N.   How many vertices does a tetrahedron have? _____

Name: _____ Date: _____

Compare space figures/Build a model   **Level:** 5 6 7 8

Triangular Space Figures

A triangular prism has two faces that are congruent polygons. Congruent figures are exactly the same size and shape.

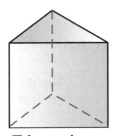

Triangular Prism

A.   What shape are the two congruent faces? _____

B.   How many faces in all? _____

C.   How many edges? _____

D.   How many vertices? _____

Compare the triangular pyramid and the rectangular pyramid.

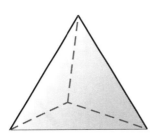

Triangular Pyramid

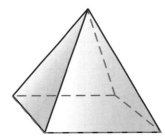

Rectangular Pyramid

		Faces	**Edges**	**Vertices**
E.	triangular pyramid	_____	_____	_____
F.	rectangular pyramid	_____	_____	_____

Imagine what one of these three space figures (triangular prism, triangular pyramid, rectangular pyramid) would look like if it were opened up and laid out flat.

G.   Make a rough draft on scrap paper. When you are certain how it would look, draw it on heavier paper, cut it out, and tape it together to make a model of the space figure.

Name: _____ Date: _____

Locate points on a grid

Level: 4   5   6   7   8

What's the Point?

You will need pencils and two dice for this two-player game.

Directions:

1. Players take turns rolling the two dice, one at a time. The number on the first die is the number for the *x*-axis. The number on the second die is the number for the *y*-axis.

2. Each player marks the point on his or her grid indicated by the two numbers on the dice. Players check each other. If the point is incorrect, the player erases and skips that turn.

3. Play continues until one player correctly marks all points on his or her grid.

Player 1

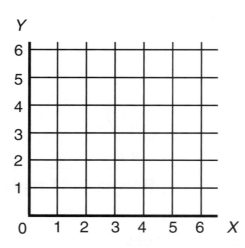

Player 2

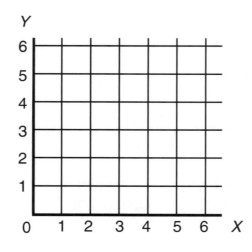

Name: _____ Date: _____

Recognition of ordered pairs in the plane   **Level:** 4 5 6 7 8

Points in the Plane

Real-world problems often involve two or more unknowns. A company's profit (*p*) may depend on its sales (*s*), or the cost (*c*) of mailing a package may depend on its weight (*w*). These types of relationships typically lead to the use of equations with two variables; for example, $3x - y = 5$. If we are to gain an understanding of these relationships, we will need an understanding of the **rectangular (or Cartesian) coordinate system**, which was named after the French mathematician, René Descartes.

This system consists of two perpendicular axes, or number lines. The horizontal line is called the **x-axis**, and the vertical is called the **y-axis**. The point where these two axes intersect is called the **origin**, which is labeled by the ordered pair (0, 0). The numbers on the axes to the right and above the origin are positive. The numbers on the axes to the left and below the origin are negative. These axes divide the rectangular plane into four parts known as **quadrants**. All of this information is labeled in the diagram at the right.

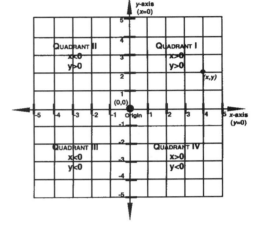

We can indicate the location of any point in the rectangular plane by the use of an **ordered pair** of the form (*x*, *y*). The x-coordinate is always placed first, and the y-coordinate always comes second. Thus, we have the significance of an ordered pair. You can remember this order easily by recalling that *x* always comes before *y* alphabetically. Notice that every ordered pair (*x*, *y*) represents one, and only one, point on the rectangular plane, and every point on the plane can be represented by one, and only one, ordered pair, (*x*, *y*).

Directions: Match each ordered pair in the list below with one of the letters that represents a point on the rectangular grid displayed at right. Be careful, because there are more letters than needed.

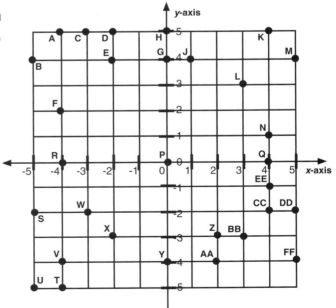

1. (-2, 5) _____   2. (1, 4) _____
3. (0, 4) _____   4. (-3, -2) _____
5. (4, 0) _____   6. (-2, -3) _____
7. (5, -2) _____   8. (4, 5) _____
9. (-4, 5) _____   10. (-4, 0) _____
11. (0, -4) _____   12. (4, 1) _____
13. (3, 3) _____   14. (-4, -4) _____
15. (3, -3) _____   16. (-5, 4) _____
17. (0, 0) _____   18. (2, -3) _____

Name: _____   Date: _____

Discover combinations to make $1/Create a chart

Level: | 4 | 5 | 6 | 7 | 8 |

Counting Coins

Directions: How many ways can you make a dollar using pennies, nickels, dimes, and quarters? Fill in the chart showing at least 20 other possibilities.

Pennies	Nickels	Dimes	Quarters
100	0	0	0
0	20	0	0
0	0	10	0
0	0	0	4

Today's Riddle: What's the quickest way to double a dollar?

Name: _____ Date: _____

Explore possible combinations

Level: ☐ 4 5 6 7 8

Decisions, Decisions

Terri wants a double dip cone with two different flavors. Before she can decide what to order, she wants to know all her options.

Her choices are:

A Choo-choo Chocolate	D Too-too Fruiti	G Purple Plum
B Razzamatazz	E Striped Delight	H Lotsa Licorice
C Very Berry	F Polka-dot Pecan	I Vanilla

Directions: Complete the chart below to show all of Terri's options for a double dip, two-flavor cone. Use the letters of the flavors.

A + B	B + C	C + ___	D + ___	E + ___	F + ___	G + ___	___ + ___	___ + ___
A + C	B + ___	C + ___	D + ___	E + ___	F + ___	G + ___	___ + ___	___ + ___
A + D	B + ___	C + ___	D + ___	E + ___	F + ___	G + ___	___ + ___	___ + ___
A + ___	B + ___	C + ___	D + ___	E + ___	F + ___	G + ___	___ + ___	___ + ___
A + ___	B + ___	C + ___	D + ___	E + ___	F + ___	G + ___	___ + ___	___ + ___
A + ___	B + ___	C + ___	D + ___	E + ___	F + ___	G + ___	___ + ___	___ + ___
A + ___	B + ___	C + ___	D + ___	E + ___	F + ___	G + ___	___ + ___	___ + ___
A + ___	B + ___	C + ___	D + ___	E + ___	F + ___	G + ___	___ + ___	___ + ___

Hint: You do not need all the spaces above. Use only the ones you need.

A. How many different options does Terri have? _____

B. What pattern did you notice as you filled in the chart?

_____

_____

_____

C. Which two flavors would you choose? _____

_____

Name: _____   Date: _____

Explore permutations   **Level:** | 4 | 5 | 6 | 7 | 8 |

Stop and Smell the Roses

Lisa has room to plant four rose bushes near the front door of her house. She wants to plant four different colored rose bushes: white, red, peach, and lavender.

Directions: Show all possible ways Lisa could arrange the roses. You can abbreviate by using "W" for white, "R" for red, "P" for peach, and "L" for lavender.

W R P L	R P L W		

Use as many of the spaces on the chart as you need. Add more spaces if needed.

A.   How many ways can Lisa arrange the four rose bushes? _____

Name: _____ Date: _____

Introduction to ordered arrangements (permutations)   **Level:**

Factorials and Permutations

Consider using an automated teller machine that uses a four-digit code. If repetition is allowed, then how many different codes are possible? The multiplication principle tells us that we have 10 choices for each digit: hence, there are $10^4 = 10,000$ different codes. What if repetition were not allowed? That is, if each of the ten digits could only be used once, how many codes are possible? Once again, use of the multiplication principle yields: $10 * 9 * 8 * 7 = 5,040$ possible codes. These ordered four-digit arrangements are called permutations.

A **permutation** is defined as any ordered arrangement of a given set of objects. When dealing with permutations, we will assume that repetition is not allowed; that is, each item is considered distinct. How many ways can we arrange the four suits in a deck of cards? The multiplication principle yields: $4 * 3 * 2 * 1 = 24$ different ways. A shorthand notation for this multiplication is called a **factorial**, hence: $4! = 4 * 3 * 2 * 1$, is read "four factorial." Most scientific calculators have the factorial (!) key, which makes for rapid calculations. It is important to note that by definition, we have the special factorial for the number zero; hence, $0! = 1$.

How many ways can eight different books be arranged from left to right on a shelf? Clearly, $8! = 40,320$. Notice that $8! = 8 * 7! = 8 * 7 * 6! = 8 * 7 * 6 * 5!$, and so forth. In general then, the number of permutations of n distinct objects is n-factorial; that is, $n!$

We can develop a formula for the first example, the 4-digit codes. Note that:

$$10 \cdot 9 \cdot 8 \cdot 7 = \frac{10 \cdot 9 \cdot 8 \cdot 7 \cdot 6 \cdot 5 \cdot 4 \cdot 3 \cdot 2 \cdot 1}{6 \cdot 5 \cdot 4 \cdot 3 \cdot 2 \cdot 1} = \frac{10!}{6!} = \frac{10!}{(10-4)!} = {}_{10}P_4$$

This symbol ${}_{10}P_4$ represents the number of permutations of ten objects taken four at a time, and the formula to its left, namely, $\frac{10!}{(10-4)!}$, tells us how to evaluate the symbol without using the multiplication property. This symbol can also be found in most scientific calculators, usually symbolized as ${}_nP_r$, where n is the number of objects to choose from and r is the number of objects chosen. Hence, our general formula for the number of permutations of r objects selected from a set of n objects is given by: ${}_nP_r = \frac{n!}{(n-r)!}$. Remember that *order* is important when using permutations.

Directions: Evaluate the following expressions:

A. ${}_6P_4$ _____

B. ${}_7P_0$ _____

C. ${}_5P_5$ _____

D. ${}_8P_3$ _____

E. If there are no ties in the final standings, how many different final standings are possible for a baseball league with 12 teams?

_____

F. In how many different ways can a gold medal, a silver medal, and a bronze medal be awarded if there are 15 competitors in the Olympic skating event?

_____

Name: _____ Date: _____

Introduction to combinations　　　　　　　　　　**Level:** ▮▮▮▮▮▮▮ 7 ▮ 8 ▮
(non-ordered arrangements)

Non-Ordered Groups

When the order of the selection of the items is important to the final outcome, the problem is best solved using permutations. When the order of the selections is unimportant to the final outcome, the problem is best solved using combinations. Hence, by definition, a **combination** is a distinct group of objects, without regard for their order or arrangement.

To highlight this difference between permutations and combinations, let's consider a group of five objects, from which we will select two objects. Suppose we let the five objects be the first five letters; that is, {a, b, c, d, e}. Write down all of the possible ordered pairs of letters. You should be able to find twenty such pairs since $_5P_2 = \frac{5!}{(5-2)!} = \frac{5!}{3!} = 5 \cdot 4 = 20$. Notice that each pair has an opposite pair consisting of the same two letters in the opposite order; for example, *be* and *eb*. Hence, it follows that there are two times as many permutations (five "pick" two) as there are combinations (five "choose" two); that is, $_5P_2 = 2 \cdot {_5C_2} = (2!) \cdot {_5C_2}$. Finally, then, we can arrive at our formula for combinations in terms of permutations given by: $_5C_2 = \frac{_5P_2}{2!} = \frac{5!}{2!3!} = 10$. Notice that we have essentially *removed the order* by dividing the number of permutations by 2. So then, in general, our formula becomes: $_nC_r = \frac{_nP_r}{r!} = \frac{n!}{r!(n-r)!}$ for *r* objects selected from *n* objects when order does not matter.

Verbally, it helps to say "*n Pick r*" for permutations, and "*n Choose r*" for combinations to help distinguish between the two symbols.

Directions: Evaluate each of the following expressions. Show your work and answers on your own paper.

A.　$\frac{7!}{5!2!}$　　　　　　B.　$\frac{9!}{7!}$　　　　　　C.　$\frac{20!}{4!16!}$

D.　In a regular poker game, five cards are randomly selected from the deck. To answer the question about how many different possible hands there are, evaluate $_{52}C_5$.

E.　If there are 100 senators at a meeting and each one will shake hands with every other senator, how many total handshakes will there be? [Hint: Evaluate $_{100}C_2$.]

F.　Suppose that there are ten cars in the running for the best car of the year. But initially, three cars are to be selected as finalists. How many ways can this initial selection occur?

G.　How many different committees can be formed from 6 teachers and 40 students, if the committee is to consist of 2 teachers and 5 students? [Hint: You will have to use the formula for combinations twice, along with the multiplication rule.]

Name: _____ Date: _____

Calculate averages/Round to nearest whole number

Level: 4 5 6 7 8

High Jinks

The High Jinks basketball team is great at basketball, but it needs a little help with math.

Directions: Calculate the average number of points for each player for the seven games. Round answers to the nearest whole numbers. Write the answers on the lines below.

Game	1	2	3	4	5	6	7
Alli G.	13	17	9	14	15	4	12
Bruno B.	14	16	11	3	8	22	9
Gorill A.	11	7	13	31	3	18	10
Pand A.	15	18	8	13	17	15	21
Leo L.	6	12	18	21	24	17	19

(Players)

A. Alli G. _____

B. Bruno B. _____

C. Gorill A. _____

D. Pand A. _____

E. Leo L. _____

Today's Riddle: Why did the chicken cross the basketball court?

Name: _____   Date: _____

Create a bar graph and a circle graph   **Level:** | 4 | 5 | 6 | 7 | 8 |

Graph It

Directions: Circle graphs and bar graphs show the same information in different ways. Use the information below to complete the exercises.

A.   Twelve children were asked how old they were when they first learned to ride a bike. Two were six, four were seven, three were eight, two were nine, and one was ten.

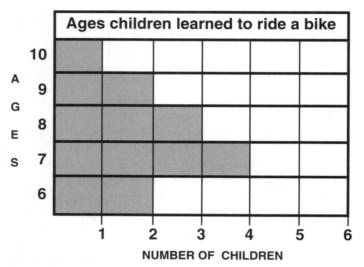

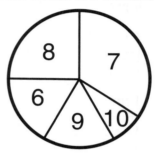

Percent of Children Who Learned to Ride a Bike at a Certain Age

Which of the two graphs do you think is easier to understand? Why?

_____

_____

B.   Twenty people were asked to name their favorite pizza topping. Complete the bar graph below to show the results of this survey.

Sausage: 5   **Pepperoni: 4**   **Canadian bacon: 3**   **Black olives: 1**
Mushrooms: 5   **Onions: 2**

Title:										
Sausage										
Pepperoni										
Canadian bacon										
Black olives										
Mushrooms										
Onions										

0   1   2   3   4   5   6   7   8   9   10

Title: _____

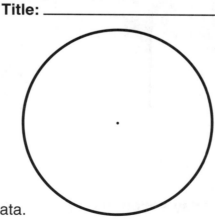

C.   Complete the circle graph at the right to show the same data.

Name: _____   Date: _____

Find averages

Level: ▮▮▮▮ 5 6 7 8

Tackle This

Directions: The 11 offensive starters are pretty big guys, but the defensive players are even bigger. Answer the following questions about the team.

	Offense Height	Weight		Defense Height	Weight
Bret	6′ 2″	225	Santana	6′ 5″	287
LeRoy	6′ 0″	204	Earl	6′ 4″	317
Antuan	6′ 1″	210	Bubba	6′ 6″	260
Bill	6′ 3″	205	Vonnie	6′ 5″	290
Ahman	6′ 0″	217	Gilbert	6′ 2″	339
Corey	6′ 1″	196	James	6′ 3″	266
Antonio	6′ 1″	198	Mike	6′ 5″	297
Frank	6′ 3″	305	Chad	6′ 5″	327
Earl	6′ 4″	317	Torrance	6′ 2″	255
Casey	6′ 1″	197	Bernardo	6′ 2″	250
Marco	6′ 4″	310	Rod	6′ 3″	320

	Offense	**Defense**

A.   Total weight   _____   _____

B.   Average weight   _____   _____
     (round to nearest pound)

C.   Average height   _____   _____
     (round to nearest inch)

D.   On the average, which group weighs more, the offense or defense? _____

E.   How much more? _____

F.   On the average, which group is taller, the offense or defense? _____

G.   How much taller? _____

Name: _____   Date: _____

Complete Venn diagrams   **Level:** ▮▮▮ 5 6 7 8

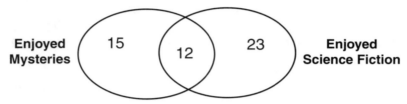

A survey showed that out of 50 people, 27 said they enjoyed mysteries, and 35 said they liked science fiction books.

Enjoyed Mysteries 15 12 23 **Enjoyed Science Fiction**

Use the Venn diagram to answer the questions.

A.   How many people enjoyed both mysteries and science fiction? _____

B.   How many enjoyed only mysteries? _____

C.   How many enjoyed only science fiction? _____

Of 84 people surveyed, 47 said they liked to eat popcorn while watching a movie, and 56 said they liked to eat chips and dip while watching a movie.

D.   Complete the Venn diagram to show the results of this survey.

Popcorn   **Chips & Dip**

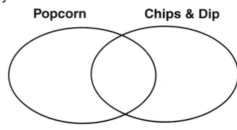

E.   How many of the people surveyed enjoyed both popcorn and chips and dip while watching a movie?

_____

Of 100 people surveyed, 53% said they owned a pair of black shoes, and 67% said they owned a pair of running shoes.

F.   Complete the Venn diagram to show the results of this survey. Include labels on the diagram.

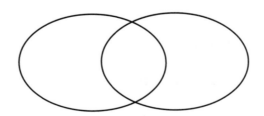

Name: _____ Date: _____

Collect data/Create a graph/Calculate percents

Level: 4 5 6 7 8

Edible Math

For this project you will need several bags of M & Ms™.

A. Work with a group. Sort the candies by colors. Fill in the table.

Color	Number

B. How many candies were there in all? _____

C. Make a graph to show how many candies of each color you have.

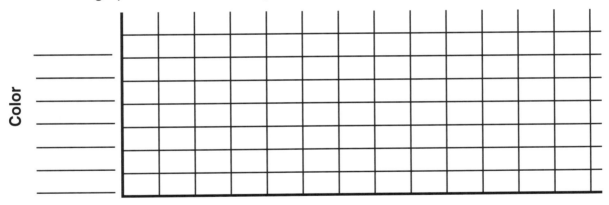

Color

25 50 75 100 125 150 175 200 225 250 275 300 325

Number

Write the answers. Round to the nearest whole percent.

D. What percent of the candies were yellow? _____

E. What percent of the candies were green? _____

F. What percent of the candies were red? _____

G. What percent of the candies were brown? _____

H. What percent of the candies were orange? _____

I. What percent of the candies were blue? _____

J. What percent of the candies were purple? _____

When you finish, enjoy the candy.

Name: _____   Date: _____

Finding the median value for a data set   **Level:** 4 5 6 7 8

The Middle of the Road

When we are asked to summarize a set of data measurements with a single number that is in some way typical of the entire distribution of measurements, we can use a measure of central tendency called the **median**. An easy way to remember how to find this number is to remember that *the median of a roadway is always in the middle.*

To find the median, we would first need to sort all of the observations in an increasing order of magnitude, and then find the middle number. For example, if the following set of numbers represents the number of home runs by eleven baseball players during the 2009 season, find the median number of home runs for these eleven players:

11, 17, 37, 35, 23, 9, 5, 14, 22, 12, 8

Remember, first we need to put these numbers in an increasing or ascending order, thus:

5, 8, 9, 11, 12, 14, 17, 22, 23, 35, 37

The middle number is 14, hence, the median number of home runs by these baseball players during the 2009 season is 14 home runs. Notice there was an *odd* number of players.

What happens if there is an *even* number of measurements or observations? For example, the following numbers are the weights of eight race car drivers:

212, 176, 203, 198, 187, 196, 209, 221

In this case, the median is the average of the middle two numbers. We again put them in order:

176, 187, 196, 198, 203, 209, 212, 221

and then take the average of 198 and 203, that is, (198 + 203) / 2, which yields a median of 200.5 pounds for the eight drivers.

Directions: Find the median value for each of the following data sets. We have left enough room for you to rewrite each set of numbers as an ordered list. Either circle the number in the set that is the median value or write your answer on the side and circle it.

A.   34, 56, 87, 52, 98, 88, 76, 74, 68, 70, 57, 91, 86, 71, 75

_____

B.   7.5, 7.6, 7.3, 7.4, 7.3, 7.6, 7.2, 7.5, 7.4, 7.6

_____

C.   190, 201, 164, 102, 95, 191, 188, 196, 110, 270, 284, 169, 105, 200

_____

D.   100, 60, 30, 40, 20, 90, 140, 40, 60, 30, 40, 50, 80

_____

E. $123.72, 96.27, 115.82, 396.81, 157.48, 131.62, 119.25, 161.59, 145.30, 106.82

_____

Name: _____ Date: _____

Finding the arithmetic mean for a data set   **Level:** | 5 | 6 | 7 | 8 |

A Mean Mentality

Another measure of central tendency for a data set is the **arithmetic mean.** The mean can be thought of as a fulcrum or balance point in the middle of the set. The mean is also known as the average. To calculate the mean, first add up all of the numbers in the data set, and then divide this total by the number of observations in the data set.

For example, if the data set consists of the five numbers, { 28, 19, 47, 34, 47 }, then the sum, denoted Σx, would be $\Sigma x = 28 + 19 + 47 + 34 + 47 = 175$. Finally, the mean, denoted by $\bar{x}$, would be calculated thusly: $\bar{x} = \dfrac{\Sigma x}{n} = \dfrac{175}{5} = 35$. Note that n represents the number of observations in the data set. In this case, n is identical with 5.

Now, if we subtract $\bar{x}$ from each data point, that is $x - \bar{x}$, for each x, and then add all of these so-called differences, the result is always the same. Try it out, and see for yourself using the data set above. [You should have found: $(-7) + (-16) + (+12) + (-1) + (+12) = 0$.] The sum of these differences is always zero, which shows that $\bar{x}$ is the balance point, or the middle of the set of data.

Directions: For each data set below, find the mean and also find the median.

		Mean	Median

A.   1.1, 4.9, 5.3, 5.9, 6.2, 6.3, 6.8, 7.6, 8.0, 8.1, 8.8

_____   _____ _____

B.   400, 950, 850, 800, 600, 1000, 850, 850, 850, 800, 850

_____   _____ _____

C.   55, 50, 53, 54, 53, 55, 56, 58, 60, 54, 54, 55, 58, 52, 54, 56, 57, 59

_____   _____ _____

D.   11, 6, 5, 1, 12, 9, 17, 4, 13, 3, 11, 10, 8, 7, 5, 4, 6, 12

_____   _____ _____

E.   1, 2, 1, 1, 1, 2, 2, 1, 1, 2, 1, 2, 2, 1, 2, 1, 2, 1, 2, 1, 2, 2, 2, 1

_____   _____ _____

Name: _____   Date: _____

Using stem-and-leaf plots to show data distribution

Level: ▓▓▓▓▓▓▓▓▓▓▓ 7 8

Visual Data Analysis

The **stem-and-leaf plot** is a method of organizing data through a combination of sorting and graphing. We use a part of each data value as a **stem** and the remaining part as the **leaf** to form groups or classes.

Consider the following twenty raw data points consisting of final exam scores: {65, 54, 76, 72, 71, 83, 72, 92, 60, 42, 73, 84, 72, 97, 72, 91, 53, 63, 84, 85}.

We will use the tens-digit of each number as the stem and the units-digit as the leaf, giving us the *unordered* stem-and-leaf plot on the left, which in turn yields the *ordered* plot on the right:

```
4 | 2                       4 | 2
5 | 4 3                     5 | 3 4
6 | 5 0 3                   6 | 0 3 5
7 | 6 2 1 2 3 2 2           7 | 1 2 2 2 2 3 6
8 | 3 4 4 5                 8 | 3 4 4 5
9 | 2 7 1                   9 | 1 2 7
```

Notice when you turn the stem-and-leaf plot on its side, you essentially have a histogram of the frequency diagram. However, what makes this type of plot special is that we have retained the raw data. Each leaf retains its identity adjacent to a specific stem. Hence, 6 | 3 = 63.

A. Now, on your own paper, draw a stem-and-leaf plot for the following data, which are the number of stories in 27 high-rise buildings in Atlanta: {54, 72, 42, 37, 41, 65, 40, 45, 33, 39, 62, 48, 52, 32, 33, 51, 55, 34, 27, 32, 53, 31, 34, 37, 50, 26, 29}.

Related samples of raw data can be compared using back-to-back stem-and-leaf plots so that the stems are shared down the middle and the leaves are arranged outward in either direction. The following data are the number of stories in 24 buildings in New Orleans: {30, 37, 35, 36, 50, 31, 34, 35, 36, 48, 28, 29, 38, 52, 28, 25, 37, 40, 58, 28, 32, 38, 40, 61}.

B. On your own paper, construct a back-to-back plot with Atlanta on the left and New Orleans on the right. Can any conclusion be made from this *double* plot?

If the range of the raw data is not sufficient to naturally use tens as the stems, then we can split the tens into two groups of fives, for example. Consider the data: {52, 62, 64, 57, 69, 58, 71, 66, 53, 57, 74, 60, 55, 67, 68, 61, 79, 64, 65, 62, 77, 62, 63, 70}. Since there are only three natural stems, namely 5, 6, and 7, we can split the stems into 5, 5*, 6, 6*, 7, and 7*, so that 5 is the stem that represents the possible leaves 0, 1, 2, 3, and 4, whereas, 5* is the stem that represents the possible leaves 5, 6, 7, 8, and 9.

C. On your own paper, construct this last stem-and-leaf plot using these six split stems and the data in the paragraph above.

Name: _____   Date: _____

Introduction of percentiles, specifically quartiles   **Level:** ▮▮▮▮▮▮▮ 7 8

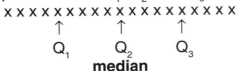

Any data set arranged in order from lowest to highest can then be divided into four groups. Three numbers or markers are needed to accomplish this procedure, and the name given to these markers is **quartiles**, represented as, Q_1, Q_2, and Q_3.

x x x x x x x x x x x x x x x x x x x x

↑   ↑   ↑

Q_1 Q_2 Q_3

median

Q_2 was introduced in The Middle of the Road activity, where we originally called it the **median**. If we use quartiles to divide the data into four groups, then Q_2 is necessarily between the two middle fourths. Once we find Q_2, it is easy to find the other quartiles by first finding the median of the lower half of the data—this will be Q_1—and then finding the median of the upper half of the data—and this will be Q_3.

Directions: Find the three quartiles for the following data set: { 11, 16, 25, 18, 9, 20, 32, 15, 20, 21 }.

A. $Q_1 =$ _____   B. $Q_2 =$ _____   C. $Q_3 =$ _____

An **outlier** is an extremely high or extremely low data value when compared to the rest of the data values as a group. A decisive method to determine which values are in the extreme in either direction starts by determining the **interquartile range (IQR)**, which is defined as **IQR** $= Q_3 - Q_1$.

Next, we multiply the **IQR** by 1.5 to set up the length of our tails. The lower tail is the distance from Q_1 that will be a limit for extreme low values, namely, $Q_1 - 1.5 \times$ **IQR**. The distance from Q_3 that will be a limit for extreme high values is $Q_3 + 1.5 \times$ **IQR**. Any data value that is outside the range of these two tails is then considered to be an *official* outlier.

D.   Are there any data values in the data set above that can now be classified as outliers?

_____

There are no strict rules on what to do with outliers. Nonetheless, when we suspect their presence, we need to check for an error of measurement or for an error in recording or transcribing any measurement. If no errors are found, then a decision has to be made as to what will be done with the outliers when further analysis of the data is expected.

Directions: For each data set below, identify the quartiles, the **IQR**, the tails, and any outliers. Record the answers in a chart on your own paper.

E.   { 242, 221, 225, 218, 230, 219 }

F.   { 33, 38, 43, 30, 29, 40, 51, 27, 42, 23, 31 }

G.   { 51, 37, 43, 49, 48, 77, 45, 92, 55, 29, 53, 59, 41, 49, 57, 17, 64, 57, 88, 46, 54 }

Name: _____ Date: _____

Calculate probability

Level: | 4 | 5 | 6 | 7 | 8

What Are the Odds?

If you turned these cards upside down and mixed them up, you would have one chance in four of turning over a heart.

A.   If the first card you turned over was not a heart, what would be your chance of drawing a heart the next time you turned over a card?

_____

B.   If you picked one card without looking from this set, what would be the chance of getting a heart? _____

C.   What would be the chance of getting a king? _____

D.   If the first card you turned over was a king, what would be the chance of turning over a queen on the next card? _____

E.   In a full deck with 52 cards, your chance of drawing a jack would be 4 out of 52. Why?

_____

_____

F.   In a full deck, what would be your chance of drawing a heart? _____

Shuffle a full deck of cards (no jokers). Turn over 28 cards, one at a time. Make tally marks to show the suit of the cards you turned over.

		Total
♣ Clubs		
♠ Spades		
♥ Hearts		
♦ Diamonds		

G.   After 28 cards, the odds are that you would have 7 of each suit. Of the four suits, which came closest to the odds? _____

Name: _____ Date: _____

Calculate probability   **Level:** | 4 | 5 | 6 | 7 | 8 |

What Are the Chances?

Directions: Answer the following questions dealing with the probability of an event occurring.

If you flip a coin, the chances are one in two that the coin will land on heads. The chance of the coin landing on heads can be expressed as a ratio **1:2**.

A.   If four chips, (red, blue, green, and white) are in a bag, the chance of selecting a white one without looking would be one in _____.   The ratio would be: _____

B.   When you roll one die, what are the chances of rolling a three? _____
The ratio would be: _____

C.   When you roll two dice, what are the chances that one of the numbers will be a three?
_____   The ratio would be: _____

D.   Four chips are in a bag (2 white and 2 black). Use pictures to show all possible combinations that could occur if you selected two chips without looking.

E.   Use your drawings. What are your chances of selecting two white chips without looking?
_____   The ratio would be: _____

F.   Use your drawings. What are the chances of selecting two chips the same color without looking? _____   The ratio would be: _____

G.   Put two white and two black chips in a bag. Select two chips without looking. Record the combination you drew. Put the chips back and repeat for a total of ten times.

_____

How did your results compare to the probability of selecting two chips of the same color?

_____

_____

Name: _____ Date: _____

Introducing the relative frequency model of probability   **Level:** [4 5 6 7 8]

Empirical Probability

Probability can be classified as either *empirical* or *theoretical*. **Empirical** means "derived from experiment or observation." **Theoretical** means "derived from mathematical analysis." The probability of an event, E, is represented by the symbol $P(E)$. The probability of an event, whether empirical or theoretical, is always a number between 0 and 1 and may be expressed as a decimal, a fraction, or a percent.

An empirical probability of 0 indicates that the event has never occurred, whereas an empirical probability of 1 indicates that the event has always occurred. An empirical event with a probability of 1 is the sun rising in the morning. An example of an empirical event with a probability of 0 is seeing a red raven.

Probabilities are never negative and never greater than one. To compute an empirical probability, or relative frequency, we simply divide the number of times that the event E has occurred by the total number of times that the experiment has been performed, that is:

$$P(E) = \frac{number\ of\ times\ event\ E\ has\ occurred}{total\ number\ of\ observations.}$$

For example, suppose that we tossed a *fair* coin 50 times, and it landed heads-up 28 times. Then, the empirical probability of the event, E = heads-up, is $P(E) = \frac{28}{50} = 0.56$. We would, in theory, expect a fair coin to land heads-up 50% of the time. In our example, we observed heads-up 56% of the time. If we continued tossing the coin many, many more times, we would see that the empirical probability of heads-up would converge ever closer to the theoretical probability of 50%. This is an illustration of the Law of Large Numbers, which states that theoretical probability statements apply, *in practice*, to a large number of trials—not to a single trial or a small number of trials.

Empirical probabilities are used every day in Gallup polls, in weather predictions, in sports, or wherever someone is keeping track of events that are occurring with regularity. Hence, empirical probabilities are subject to change over time. If you are a baseball fan, you are aware that your favorite hitter's batting average—his relative frequency of success—changes by small increments on a daily basis.

A.   If Bobby planted 100 carrot seeds in his garden last year, and 75 actually germinated, then how many seeds should Bobby plant this year if he wants to grow 300 carrots? [Hint: You will need to do some algebra with this one. Remember that 300 represents the number of successes of the event.]

_____

In a survey of 1,600 people who were randomly selected to rate the mayor's performance, 380 said the performance was good, 602 said it was fair, 490 said it was poor, and 128 had no opinion. If this sample is representative of the town's population, find the empirical probability that the next person randomly interviewed:

B.   will rate the mayor's performance as fair; or   C.   will have an opinion.

_____   _____

Name: _____ Date: _____

Exploring the classical assignment of probabilities   **Level:** 4   5   6   7   8

Equally-Likely

Theoretical probability can be determined by studying the set of all the outcomes that are possible for any given experiment. This set is called a **sample space**, and each outcome is assumed to be **equally likely**; that is, each has the same probability of occurring. For example, if we consider the experiment of flipping a *fair* coin, we could assume that the probability of landing heads and the probability of landing tails are both one-half, or 50%, without even flipping the coin.

We define the probability of an event, *E*, to be the following:

$$P(E) = \frac{number\ of\ successful\ outcomes}{total\ number\ of\ possible\ outcomes}$$

Consider the experiment of randomly drawing one card from a regular shuffled bridge deck of 52 cards with the four suits: spades, hearts, diamonds, and clubs—no jokers, of course. If an event is a subset of a sample space, that is, an event can consist of more than one outcome, use the idea of equally-likely outcomes to find the probability of each of the following events:

A.   drawing a red card _____   B.   drawing a spade _____

C.   not drawing a spade _____   D.   drawing an ace _____

E.   drawing a face card (king, queen, or jack) _____

F.   not drawing an ace _____   G.   drawing a black ten _____

Remember that we are looking to find a fraction where the numerator represents the number of outcomes that indicate a successful draw, and the denominator represents the total number of possible outcomes. You should have recognized that the denominator for all the events above is equal to 52.

Suppose that a top hat contains 12 red, 15 green, 21 blue, 9 yellow, and 3 white marbles, in total. Furthermore, suppose that one marble is randomly selected from the top hat. Can you find the probability for each of the following events?

First, you have to find the common denominator for each fraction, namely H. _____.

I.   selecting a white marble _____   J.   not selecting a green marble _____

K.   selecting a blue or a yellow marble _____   L.   selecting a red marble _____

M.   selecting any one except a yellow marble _____

N.   selecting a marble whose color has five letters _____

Processes and formulas

For Quick Reference

Keep this guide in your math folder for quick reference in case you forget a process or formula.

Working With Fractions:

Add: Convert fractions to equivalent fractions with common denominators. Add numerators.

Subtract: Convert fractions to equivalent fractions with common denominators. Subtract numerators.

Multiply: Multiply the numerators. Multiply the denominators.

Divide: Invert the second fraction and multiply.

Working With Positive and Negative Numbers:

The product of two positive or two negative numbers is a positive number.

The product of a positive and a negative number is a negative number.

The quotient of two positive or two negative numbers is a positive number.

The quotient of a positive and a negative number is a negative number.

Formulas:

Perimeter of any geometric figure with straight sides: sum of all sides

Area of square or rectangle: lw (l = length and w = width)

Area of triangle: $\frac{1}{2}bh$ (b = base and h = height)

Area of a parallelogram: bh (b = base and h = height)

Area of circle: πr^2 (π = 3.14 and r = radius)

Circumference of a circle: πd (π = 3.14 and d = diameter)

Volume of a cube or rectangular prism: lwh (l = length, w = width, h = height)

Volume of a sphere: $\frac{4}{3}\pi r^3$ (π = 3.14 and r = radius)

Volume of a cylinder: bh (b = area of base and h = height)

Volume of a cone: $\frac{1}{3}\pi r^2 h$ (π = 3.14, r = radius, h = height)

Processes, formulas, and definitions

For Quick Reference (cont.)

Data Analysis and Probability:

Combinations: The order of the group is <u>not</u> important. If r items are selected from a set of n items, then there are $_nC_r$ possible groups, where $_nC_r = \dfrac{n!}{(n-r)! \cdot r!}$.

Empirical probability: $P(E) = \dfrac{number\ of\ times\ event\ E\ has\ occurred}{total\ number\ of\ observations}$

Equally likely: Each outcome has the same probability of occurring.

Factorials: $n! = n \cdot (n-1) \cdot (n-2) \ldots (3) \cdot (2) \cdot (1)$ and by definition: $0! = 1$.

Interquartile range (IQR): This is the difference between Q_3 and Q_1. **IQR = Q_3 - Q_1**

Lower tail: This is the distance from Q_1 that is the limit for extreme low values. **Q_1 - 1.5 x IQR**

Mean (Average): Divide the sum of all the data values by how many there are. Also symbolized by $\overline{x}$.

Median: If there is an odd number of data values, use the middle value. If there is an even number of data values, use the average of the two middle values.

Outlier: This is an extremely high or extremely low data value when compared to the rest of the data values as a group.

Permutations: The order of the arrangement is important. If r items are selected from a set of n items, then there are $_nP_r$ possible arrangements, where $_nP_r = \dfrac{n!}{(n-r)!}$.

Prime numbers: A prime is divisible only by one and itself.

Quartiles: These are markers that divide a data set into four groups; Q_1, Q_2, Q_3.

Sample space: This is the set of all the outcomes that are possible for any given experiment.

Theoretical probability: $P(E) = \dfrac{number\ of\ successful\ outcomes\ for\ event\ E}{total\ number\ of\ possible\ outcomes}$

Upper tail: This is the distance from Q_3 that is the limit for extreme high values. **Q_3 + 1.5 x IQR**

Answer Keys

Simply A-Mazing (p. 2)

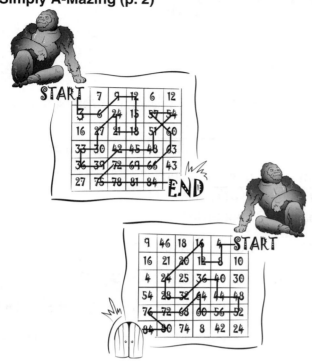

Riddle Answer: Because he had planted watermelons.

Riddle Me (p. 3)

1. It had problems.   2. Five out of three

Prime Time (p. 4)

C. Yes, It can only be evenly divided by one and itself.
D. No, It can be divided by two.
F. Prime numbers are: 1, 2, 3, 5, 7, 11, 13, 17, 19, 23, 29, 31, 37, 41, 43, 47, 53, 59, 61, 67, 71, 73, 79, 83, 89, 97

Brrrr! (p. 5)

A. 1. Minneapolis (-21), 2. Detroit (-14), 3. Boston (-11), 4. Chicago (-6), 5. Pittsburgh (3)
B. < C. > D. > E. < F. > G. >
H. -7 -6 0 2 3 4
I. -12 -9 -8 0 1 4 6
J. -8 -6 -3 2 4 5 7
K. -3 -5 -7   L. 1 3 5
M. -10 -15 -20   N. 0 5 10

Commas Help (p. 6)

A. $53,563 B. 284,164 C. 1,369,001
D. $20,460,159 E. 4,326,890 F. 901,267,891
G. $5,347; ($53,447) H. (514,222;) 51,422
I. 1,657,801; (16,578,011)
J. $43,789.08; ($43,799.08)
K. 9,235,994; (92,359,994)
L. (231,078,467;) 23,107,864
M. 35,600,000 N. $5,216 O. 87,000,907

Place Value Puzzle (p. 7)

A. 3	0	6	C. 9		D. 2	E. 7	0
O		F. 1	0		G. 8	1	
H. 4	I. 2	0	0	J. 7		K. 4	L. 6
M. 9	0	7	0	3		N. 7	4
O. 5	3		P. 6	0	Q. 3	0	3
R. 3	5		S. 9	2	4	1	0
	T. 6	U. 8		V. 8	2		1
W. 2	3	2		X. 9	0	0	9

Get the Point? (p. 10)

	Millions	Hundred Thousands	Ten Thousands	Thousands	Hundreds	Tens	Ones	Tenths	Hundredths	Thousandths	Ten-thousandths	Hundred thousandths	Millionths
A.	4	3	5	6	0	8	7	. 0	1				
B.	2	0	0	0	0	0	7	.					
C.		4	0	0	9	7	2	. 1	4	6	9		
D.							0	. 4	5	7			
E.			3	2	7	1	. 5	7	0	1	5	4	
F.					2	6	. 5	7					
G.							0	. 5	9	2	1	8	6
H.							0	. 0	0	0	0	0	3
I.		2	3	4	5	6	7	. 1	2	3	4	5	
J.	7	0	0	0	0	0	0	. 1					
K.	1	0	0	7	1	0	0	. 0	0	7	0	0	7
L.			6	2	5	6	. 1	8	7	3	5	6	

What Should You Do? (p. 11)

1. D: 1,307,985 ÷ 57
2. A: 45 + 28 + 59 + 74 + 126 + 184 + 201
3. S: 457 - 217   4. M: 7 x 15   5. M: 4 x 31
6. S: 11:30 - 8:20   7. M: 18 x 6
8. S: $10.00 - $3.05

What's Missing? (p. 12)

A. + B. ÷ C. +, +   D. -, +   E. x
F. ÷ G. -, - H. +   I. x, x J. -, +
K. ÷ L. +, -, + or -, +, -
Riddle Answer: A yardstick

Finish the Fact Families (p. 13)
B. 3; 3; 3; 3 C. 6; 6; 6; 6 D. 20; 4; 4; 5
E. 6; 6; 6; 6 F. 8; 8; 8; 8
G. 9; 9 x 8; 8 = 9; 9 = 8 H. 7; 8 x 7; 7 = 8; 8 = 7
I. 8; 8 x 6; 6 = 8; 8 = 6 J. 7; 7 x 6; 6 = 7; 7 = 6
K. 9; 9 x 7; 7 = 9; 9 = 7
L. 12; 12 x 5; 5 = 12; 12 = 5
M. 4; 3 x 4; 3 = 4; 4 = 3 N. 5; 9 x 5; 5 = 9; 9 = 5
O. 11; 11 x 9; 9 = 11; 11 = 9

Mystery Squares (p. 14)
A.

X	4	6	8	10	12
3	12	18	24	30	36
4	16	24	32	40	48
5	20	30	40	50	60
7	28	42	56	70	84
9	36	54	72	90	108

B.

−	231	622	409	713	561
45	186	577	364	668	516
56	175	566	353	657	505
63	168	559	346	650	498
72	159	550	337	641	489
81	150	541	328	632	480

C.

+	70	82	96	106	118
105	175	187	201	211	223
110	180	192	206	216	228
120	190	202	216	226	238
125	195	207	221	231	243
130	200	212	226	236	248

D.

+	6.7	8.4	3.8	2.4	7.1
1.2	7.9	9.6	5	3.6	8.3
2.3	9	10.7	6.1	4.7	9.4
3.4	10.1	11.8	7.2	5.8	10.5
4.5	11.2	12.9	8.3	6.9	11.6
5.6	12.3	14	9.4	8	12.7

Historical Math (p. 15)
A. 3,293.3 pcs. B. $16/week C. 83.5 mph
D. 3.3 mph E. 57 days F. 30.4 mph
G. 2,592 points

Body Math (p. 16)
A. 72 B. Answers will vary.
C. Answers will vary.
D. 168 miles E. 7 miles F. 32 months
G. 292 months (24.3 years)
H. 1,000 weeks (19.2 years)

At the End of the Rainbow (p. 17)
A. 24 B. 28 C. 29 D. 21
E. 40 F. 100 G. 1,000 H. 30
Riddle Answer: Nine

Cricket Math (p. 19)
A. 55 degrees B. 61 degrees
C. 6 degrees D. 28 times

Temperature	# of Chirps	Temperature	# of Chirps
45	8	46	9
50	13	49	12
54	17	53	16
56	19	58	21
60	23	64	27
63	26	69	32
66	29	70	33
67	30	72	35
72	35	75	38
73	36	77	40
76	39	79	42
79	42	80	43

A Long Way Down (p. 20)
Riddle answer: One, if it is 93 million miles long.

Hot and Cold (p. 21)
A. Like a number line, the numbers on a thermom-
   eter are in order from lowest to highest.
B. 25° C. 45° D. 40° E. 5°
F. 30° G. 55° H. 60° I. 85°
J. 5° K. 45° L. 65° M. 35°

Multiple Multiples (p. 24)
1–5. Teacher check.
A. 15, 30, 45, 60, 75, 90
B. Only 77 is a multiple of both 7 and 11.
C. Only 99 is a multiple of both 9 and 11.
D. No number between 1 and 100 is a multiple
   of 3, 5, 7, 9, and 11.

Hop to It (p. 28)
A. 21 ÷ 7 = 3 B. 16 ÷ 4 = 4
C. 54 ÷ 6 = 9 D. 30 ÷ 6 = 5
E. 56 ÷ 7 = 8 F. 42 ÷ 7 = 6
G. 63 ÷ 9 = 7 H. 64 ÷ 8 = 8
I. 36 ÷ 4 = 9 J. 28 ÷ 4 = 7
K. 27 ÷ 9 = 3 L. 24 ÷ 6 = 4
M. 54 ÷ 9 = 6 N. 40 ÷ 5 = 8
O. 35 ÷ 5 = 7

No Remainders (p. 31)
A. 3, 6, 9, 12, 15, 18, 21, 24, 27, 30, 33, 36, 39,
   42, 45, 48, 51, 54, 57, 60, 63, 66, 69, 72, 75,
   78, 81, 84, 87, 90, 93, 96, 99
B. 8, 16, 24, 32, 40, 48, 56, 64, 72, 80, 88, 96
C. 7, 14, 21, 28, 35, 42, 49, 56, 63, 70, 77, 84, 91,
   98

D. 5, 10, 15, 20, 25, 30, 35, 40, 45, 50, 55, 60, 65, 70, 75, 80, 85, 90, 95, 100
E. 15, 21, 24, 30, 35, 40, 42, 45, 48, 56, 60, 63, 70, 72, 75, 80, 84, 90, 96
F. 35 and 70
G. 24, 48, 72, 96
H. None

Fraction Collections (p. 33)

Tori's Fractions: $\frac{2}{3}$; $\frac{7}{8}$; $\frac{9}{12}$; $\frac{8}{9}$; $\frac{15}{16}$; $\frac{17}{32}$; $\frac{4}{5}$; $\frac{7}{10}$; $\frac{3}{8}$

Taj's Fractions: $\frac{7}{6}$; $\frac{6}{4}$; $\frac{8}{3}$; $\frac{18}{6}$; $\frac{99}{97}$; $\frac{4}{3}$; $\frac{2}{1}$

Devan's Fractions: $1\frac{3}{4}$; $9\frac{1}{8}$; $6\frac{4}{7}$; $5\frac{7}{10}$; $4\frac{1}{9}$; $16\frac{1}{16}$; $8\frac{7}{8}$; $1\frac{99}{99}$; $2\frac{5}{6}$

Balancing Act (p. 34)

A. $\frac{1}{2}$ B. $\frac{8}{10}$ or $\frac{4}{5}$ C. $\frac{1}{4}$ D. $\frac{1}{10}$
E. 0.5   F. 0.6   G. 0.5 or 0.50 H. 0.75

Bull's-eye (p. 35)

A.    B.

C.    D.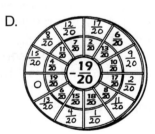

Show Me (p. 36)

Teacher check to make sure the correct number of tenths is shaded.

Sock Sort (p. 37)

A. $1\frac{4}{5}$ B. $1\frac{1}{4}$ C. $3\frac{3}{4}$ D. $5\frac{2}{3}$
E. $2\frac{4}{7}$ F. $2\frac{2}{3}$ G. $1\frac{1}{3}$ H. $1\frac{4}{7}$
I. $5\frac{1}{3}$ J. $2\frac{4}{5}$ K. $4\frac{1}{2}$ L. $2\frac{1}{2}$
M. $1\frac{1}{5}$ N. $2\frac{1}{5}$ O. $1\frac{1}{6}$ P. $1\frac{1}{2}$
Q. $1\frac{2}{3}$ R. $2\frac{1}{10}$ S. $16\frac{2}{3}$ T. $2\frac{2}{5}$

Ordering and Adding (p. 38)

A, D, F, G, H, C, E, B
I. $\frac{5}{6}$ J. $\frac{7}{12}$ K. $1\frac{1}{3}$ L. $\frac{1}{2}$ M. $\frac{11}{16}$

Alien Survey (p. 40)

	Fraction:	Decimal:	Ratio:
A.	$\frac{2}{5}$	0.4	4:10
B.	$\frac{3}{10}$	0.3	3:10
C.	$\frac{3}{5}$	0.6	6:10
D.	$\frac{1}{2}$	0.5	6:12
E.	$\frac{1}{4}$	0.25	25:100
F.	$\frac{13}{100}$	0.13	13:100
G.	$\frac{1}{4}$	0.25	4:16
H.	$\frac{3}{4}$	0.75	9:12
I.	$\frac{7}{20}$	0.35	350:1000

Big Tippers (p. 41)

A. $1.57   B. $3.91   C. $2.67   D. $1.69
E. $1.58   F. $3.58   G. $1.65   H. $1.22
I. $2.34   J. $2.53

Tax on Tacks (p. 42)

A. $0.40; $10.39   B. $7.79; $137.65
C. $38.68; $812.36   D. $1.80; $31.75
E. $1.22; $18.60   F. $0.09; $2.07
G. $3.75; $72   H. $1,294.74; $22,873.74

At the Factor-E (p. 43)

A. 6   B. 24 C. 45 D. 18 E. 40 F. 21
G. 36 H. 15 I. 56 J. 24 K. 30

Snakes and Snails and Puppy Dog Tails (p. 46)

A. $\frac{1}{3}$ of the class   B. $\frac{5}{6}$ pound   C. $1\frac{7}{16}$ pounds
D. $\frac{2}{9}$ quart   E. 15 inches
F. NEW RECIPE:
    $1\frac{2}{3}$ pounds crunchy ants
    $2\frac{3}{16}$ pounds peanut shells
    $4\frac{3}{8}$ pounds chocolate-covered crickets
    $\frac{5}{16}$ pound snails with shell
    $5\frac{15}{16}$ pounds honey
    $1\frac{1}{9}$ pounds chopped beetles

Web Divide (p. 47)

A. 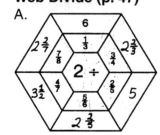   B.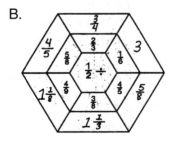

C. 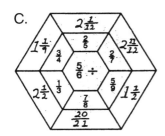   D. 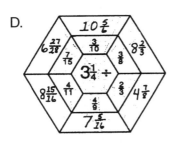   **Beware of Triangles (p. 55)**

Music to My Ears (p. 49)

A. 5%, 0.05, $\frac{1}{20}$ B. 6%, 0.06, $\frac{3}{50}$
C. 1%, 0.01, $\frac{1}{100}$ D. 13%, 0.13, $\frac{13}{100}$
E. 11%, 0.11, $\frac{11}{100}$ F. 7%, 0.07, $\frac{7}{100}$
G. 58%, 0.58, $\frac{29}{50}$ H. 30%, 0.3, $\frac{3}{10}$
I. 12%, 0.12, $\frac{3}{25}$

Seeing Stars (p. 51)

A. 16 B. 11 C. 9 D. 10 E. 4

Cookie Caper (p. 52)

Move the bottom cookie so it sits on top of the one above it. That will give two rows of cookies with four in each row. (You can also move the top cookie to sit on top of the middle cookie.)
Riddle answer: The 11 they didn't eat.

Coin Tricks (p. 53)

A. Move one penny from Julie to Jessica. Move one dime from Jessica to Julie.
B. Both now have 46 cents.
C. Four dimes and two nickels; one quarter and five nickels
D. 14 cents
Riddle Answer: It has more cents (sense).

Fence It In (p. 54)

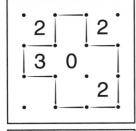 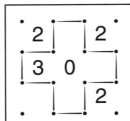

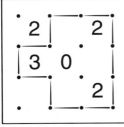

Welcome to Rainbow Apartments (p. 56)

Fifth floor: yellow
Fourth floor: pink
Third floor: blue
Second floor: lavender
First floor: green

Brain Teasers (p. 57)

A. The bun costs 10 cents.
B. Tina is 18 and Marco is 6.
C. Four minutes. (Each carpenter takes four minutes to nail up one sheet of paneling.)
D. 108 books in all
E. Stephanie has 8 and Trevor has 4. If she gives him 2, they will both have 6.
F. The numbers from 0 to 100 contain 50 pairs that add up to 100.
100 + 0, 99 + 1, 98 + 2, 97 + 3, etc. and the number 50 is an unpaired leftover. 50 x 100 = 5,000 + 50 = 5,050

Pick Up Sticks (p. 58)

A.   B.

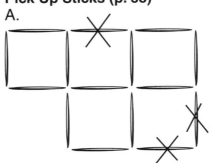   

Banner Day (p. 59)

A.

	Red	Gold	Blue
Anna	4'	$2\frac{1}{2}$'	30"
Barb	48"	24"	3'
Carrie	42"	38"	28"

B. Move the 18 to the first streamer and the numbers in all streamers will add up to 30.

Master Math Challenges (p. 60)

A. Abby - 62; Brett - 69; Luis - 67; Mia - 71; Tomás - 58
B. 51 leaves in all. The 4' beanstalk had 10 leaves, the 6' beanstalk had 16 leaves, and the 9' beanstalk had 25 leaves.
C. 20 dragons   D.   24 riders

Twins Convention (p. 61)

A. Anna and Bob arrived on Monday.
B. Beth and Sam arrived on Friday.
C. Dana and Cal arrived on Wednesday.
D. Ellen and Nick arrived on Thursday.
E. Jill and Al arrived on Tuesday.

	Al	Bob	Cal	Nick	Sam	Mon	Tue	Wed	Thu	Fri
Anna	N	Y	N	N	N	Y	N	N	N	N
Beth	N	N	N	N	Y	N	N	N	N	Y
Dana	N	N	Y	N	N	N	N	Y	N	N
Ellen	N	N	N	Y	N	N	N	N	Y	N
Jill	Y	N	N	N	N	N	Y	N	N	N
Mon	N	Y	N	N	N					
Tue	Y	N	N	N	N					
Wed	N	N	Y	N	N					
Thu	N	N	N	Y	N					
Fri	N	N	N	N	Y					

Party Time (p. 62)

Rob	Carlson	Cleaned up	Green
Tina	O'Brien	Invitations	Blue
Maria	Edwards	Decorated	Purple
Carlos	Juarez	Made food	Red

Brain Benders (p. 63)

A. 49 + 50 + 51
B. Scott is 6' 9" and Tyrone is 6' 7".
C. Harry is 6, Henry is 2, and Hannah is 8.
D. 3 school buses
E. Bus 1: 32, Bus 2: 36, Bus 3: 42.
   Total: 110 passengers
F. Jason is 16. (His grandfather is 64.)
G. Combinations: 12

Hattie's Hat Sale (p. 64)

A. $16.96   B. $94.51   C. $134.32
D. $21.90   E. $28.30   F. $9.89
G. $9.09   H. $109.66   I. $14.13
J. $18.48

Comparing Costs (p. 65)

A. 6 cans   B. 3 cans   C. 6 pounds
D. 5 pounds   E. 10 apples   F. 3 pens
G. 6 folders   H. 12 bottles   I. 50 pounds
J. 1 pound   K. 18 eggs   L. 1 gallon
M. 12 buns   N. 2 pounds

Help Wanted (p. 66)

Abby $462.25   Ben $650.00
Carlos $719.63   Dana $484.93
Eduardo $630.19
A. 44   B. $512.88   C. $2,027.04
D. and E. Answers will vary. Option 2 allows workers to earn more money per two-weeks. Option 1 requires longer work days, but more days off.

Just Passing Time (p. 68)

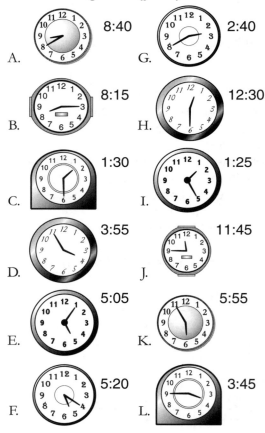

A. 8:40
G. 2:40
B. 8:15
H. 12:30
C. 1:30
I. 1:25
D. 3:55
J. 11:45
E. 5:05
K. 5:55
F. 5:20
L. 3:45

Rock Around the Clock (p. 69)

A. 3 hours, 45 minutes   B. 4 hours, 35 minutes
C. 10 hours, 5 minutes   D. 11 hours, 5 minutes
E. 7 hours, 35 minutes   F. 4 hours, 55 minutes
G. 6 hours, 50 minutes   H. 12 hours, 5 minutes
I. 22 hours, 25 minutes J. 8 hours, 10 minutes
K. 18 hours, 10 minutes L. 12 hours, 30 minutes

Step by Step (p. 70)
A. 5 B. 1 C. 4 D. 3 E. 6 F. 2
G. Teacher check.
H.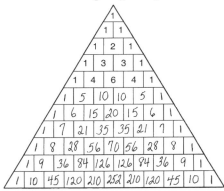

Riddle Answer: None; The dirt has already been removed.

Sheila Sees Seashells by the Seashore (p. 71)

Triangle	1	2	3	4	5	6
Number of shells on each side	2	3	4	5	6	7
Total number of shells	3	6	9	12	15	18

Super Challenge: 21 seashells on each side, 60 seashells in all

Pascal's Triangle (p. 72)

```
            1
           1 1
          1 2 1
         1 3 3 1
        1 4 6 4 1
       1 5 10 10 5 1
      1 6 15 20 15 6 1
     1 7 21 35 35 21 7 1
    1 8 28 56 70 56 28 8 1
   1 9 36 84 126 126 84 36 9 1
  1 10 45 120 210 252 210 120 45 10 1
```

A Non-Stop Difference (p. 73)
A. 63, 75, 87, 99, 111 common difference = 12
B. 349, 427, 505, 583, 661 common difference = 78
C. 13, -4, -21, -38, -55 common difference = -17
D.
```
 1   5   12   22   35   51   70   92   117
   4   7   10   13   16   19   22   25
     3   3   3   3   3   3   3
```
E.
```
-7   -2   8   23   43   68   98   133   173
   5   10   15   20   25   30   35   40
     5   5   5   5   5   5   5
```
F.
```
1   5   14   30   55   91   140   204   285
  4   9   16   25   36   49   64   81
    5   7   9   11   13   15   17
      2   2   2   2   2   2
```

A Non-Stop Product (p. 74)
A. 2401, 16807, 117649 common ratio = 7
B. 324, -972, 2916   common ratio = -3
C. 3, 1, 1/3   common ratio = 1/3
D. -1/8, 1/32, -1/128   common ratio = -1/4
E. 64, 256/3, 1024/9   common ratio = 4/3
F. -81/4, 243/8, -729/16 common ratio = -3/2
G. 42, 56, 72, 90   Algebraic
H. -16/81, 32/243, -64/729, 128/2187 Geometric
I. 75, 99, 123, 147   Arithmetic
J. 36 $\sqrt{3}$, -108, 108 $\sqrt{3}$, -324   Geometric

Happily Ever After (p. 75)
Check answers based on numbers students used.
Answers will vary.
First task: 29 piles of 11 or 11 piles of 29.
Second task: 17 24 19
               22 20 18
               21 16 23

Tic-Tac-Go (page 76)

A.
4	39	3
7	7	0
2	6	12

B.
8	4	7
12	1	5
10	3	10

C.
3	6	12
5	7	11
12	222	7

D.
4	81	7
54	10	88
25	72	25

Let t Represent Temperature (p. 77)
A. $t + 21$
B. $6c$ or $c * 6$
C. $n + 2$
D. $w + 1, w + 2, w + 3$
E. $s - 20$
F. $h + 0.25h$ or $h + (0.25 * h)$
G. $s * 7$ or $7s$
H. $m * 0.15$ or $0.15m$

World Records (p. 79)
A. 122.66 ÷ 2 = 61.33 ft. (radius)
    61.33^2 x 3.14 = 11,810.7 sq. ft.
B. 11,810.7 - 10,057 = 1,753.7 sq. ft.
C. 134° - (-79.8°) = 213.8°
D. 40 x 23 = 920 sq. ft.
E. 40 + 40 + 23 + 23 = 126 ft.
    or 2(40) + 2(23) = 126 ft.
F. 172 ft. x 12 in. + 4 in. = 2,068 in.
G. 2,068 in. ÷ 36 in. = 57.4 yd.

Every Which Way (p. 82)
1. B   2. A   3. C
4. and 5. Teacher check.

Before the Wheel (p. 83)
A., B., C. Teacher check.

Cube It (p. 84)
A. 64 B. 4   C. 24 D. 24 E. 8

Surround It (p. 85)
A. 14 units   B. 12 units   C. 12 units
D. 12 units   E. 12 units   F. 26 units
G. 20 units   H. 22 units   I. B, C, D, and E

Area (page 86)
A. 40 sq. in. B. 36 sq. in. C. 92 sq. in.
D. rectangle and triangle; find area of each, then
    add; 136 sq. in.
E. rectangle and triangle; 60 sq. in.
F. 542 sq. in. G. 55 sq. in.

Waldo's Wonderful World of Wallpaper (p. 87)
A. 54 feet, 2 inches   B. 4 rolls
C. 182.75 square feet   D. 21 square yards
E. 43 feet, 8 inches   F. 3 rolls G. $26.91

Time for Angles (p. 88)
A. acute   B. obtuse   C. right

D. obtuse   E. obtuse   F. acute

G. acute   H. acute   I. right

Always 180° (p. 89)
A. 180°
B. Add the two angles and subtract the sum from
    180.
C. 75°   D. 60°   E. 90°   F. 20°
G. 45°   H. 150°   I. 50°   J. 70°
K. 40°

Spinning Circles (p. 90)
A. 4.5 inches   B. 12.6 inches
C. 9.4 yards   D. 18.8 inches
E. 11 feet   F. 31.4 miles
G. 44 inches   H. 25.1 feet
I. 40.8 miles
J. d = 3.4 feet; C = 10.7 feet
K. r = 5.5 inches; C = 34.5 inches
L. r = 6 miles; C = 37.7 miles
M. d = 5 miles; C = 15.7 miles

Around and Around (p. 91)
A. 23.6 in.   B. 6,780.2 mi.   C. 1,079.7 mi.
D. 785 ft.   E. 2,160   F. 1.5 mi.
G. 1,029.9 ft. H. 244.9 ft.   I. 69.1 in.
J. 9.5 ft.   K. 317.1 ft.

What's My Line? (p. 92)
A. Possible answers: $\overline{BA}$, $\overline{BC}$, $\overline{DB}$, $\overline{DE}$, $\overline{EF}$, $\overline{HD}$,
    $\overline{GH}$, $\overline{HI}$, $\overline{IJ}$, $\overline{JK}$, $\overline{KL}$, $\overline{KF}$, $\overline{FC}$
B. Possible answers: $\overleftrightarrow{BC}$, $\overleftrightarrow{DF}$, $\overleftrightarrow{GL}$, $\overleftrightarrow{HA}$, $\overleftrightarrow{CK}$
C. Possible answers: $\overrightarrow{BA}$, $\overrightarrow{DA}$, $\overrightarrow{HG}$, $\overrightarrow{FC}$, $\overrightarrow{FK}$, $\overrightarrow{EF}$,
    $\overrightarrow{ED}$, $\overrightarrow{IG}$, $\overrightarrow{IL}$, $\overrightarrow{JL}$, $\overrightarrow{KL}$
D. Intersecting   E. Perpendicular
F. Parallel   G. Intersecting

Triangle Tango (p. 93)
A. No. The three angles of an equilateral triangle
    are equal. A right triangle has one angle of 90°.
    Since the sum of the three angles equals 180°,
    a triangle with three 90° angles is impossible.
B. Yes. Drawings may vary.
    Here is one example.

C. Drawings may vary. Here is
    one example.

D. Here is an example.

These Space Figures Aren't From Mars (p. 94)
A. No   B. Yes   C. Yes
D. Tetrahedron, octahedron, and icosahedron
E. Cube   F. Dodecahedron
G. 6   H. 4   I. Answers will vary
J. 12   K. 6   L. 30   M. 8   N. 4

Triangular Space Figures (p. 95)
A. triangular B. 5 C. 9 D. 6 E. 4; 6; 4
F. 5; 8; 5

Points in the Plane (p 97)
1. D   2. J   3. G   4. W   5. Q   6. X
7. DD 8. K   9. A   10. R 11. Y 12. N
13. L 14. V 15. BB 16. B 17. P 18. Z

Counting Coins (p. 98)
Teacher check combinations.
Riddle Answer: Fold it in half

Decisions, Decisions (p. 99)
A. There are 36 options.
B. The number of options for each column is one
   less than the previous column.

Stop and Smell the Roses (p. 100)
There are 24 possible choices.

Factorials and Permutations (p. 101)
A. 360   B. 1   C. 120   D. 336
E. 12! = 479,001,600   F. 2730

Non-ordered Groups (p. 102)
A. 21   B. 72   C. 4845 D. 2,598.960
E. 4,950 F. 120   G. 9,870,120

High Jinks (p. 103)
A. Alli G. 12   B. Bruno B. 12
C. Gorill A. 13   D. Pand A. 15
E. Leo L. 17
Riddle Answer: The referee called fowl!

Graph It (p. 104)
A. Answers will vary, but will probably be the bar
   graph because it is more exact.
B. and C. Teacher check graphs.

Tackle This (p. 105)
A. Offense: 2,584 pounds;
   Defense: 3,208 pounds
B. Offense: 235 pounds; Defense: 292 pounds
C. Offense: 6′ 2″; Defense: 6′ 4″
D. Defense   E. 57 pounds
F. Defense   G. 2 inches

Surveys Show (p. 106)
A. 12 B. 15 C. 23
D.

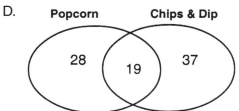

E. 19
F.

Owned   Owned
Black Shoes   Running Shoes

33   (20)   47

The Middle of the Road (p. 108)
A. 74   B. 7.45   C. 189   D. 50
E. 127.67

A Mean Mentality (p. 109)
A. 6.27, 6.3 B. 800, 850   C. 55.167, 55
D. 8, 7.5   E. 1.5, 1.5

Visual Data Analysis (p. 110)
A. Atlanta

```
2 | 6 7 9
3 | 1 2 2 3 3 4 4 7 7 9
4 | 0 1 2 5 8
5 | 0 1 2 3 4 5
6 | 2 5
7 | 2
```

B.

```
              Atlanta |   | New Orleans
                  9 7 6 | 2 | 5 8 8 8 9
      9 7 7 4 4 3 3 2 2 1 | 3 | 0 1 2 4 5 5 6 6 7 7 8 8
            8 5 2 1 0 | 4 | 0 0 8
            5 4 3 2 1 0 | 5 | 0 2 8
                  5 2 | 6 | 1
                     2 | 7 |
```

For B. above, it appears that Atlanta has the highest building and the higher ones on average.

C.

```
5  | 2 3
5* | 5 7 7 8
6  | 0 1 2 2 2 3 4 4
6* | 5 6 7 8 9
7  | 0 1 4
7* | 7 9
```

Quartiles and Outliers (p. 111)
A. $Q_1 = 15$ B. $Q_2 = 19$ C. $Q_3 = 21$
D. Yes, 32 is an outlier.
E. Q_1: 219; Q_2: 223; Q_3: 230; IQR: 11;
   Lower Tail: 202.5; Upper Tail: 246.5;
   Outlier(s): None
F. Q_1: 29: Q_2: 33; Q_3: 42; IQR: 13; Lower Tail: 9.5;
   Upper Tail: 61.5; Outlier(s): None
G. Q_1: 45; Q_2: 51; Q_3: 57; IQR: 12; Lower Tail: 27;
   Upper Tail: 75; Outliers(s): 17, 77, 88, 92

What Are the Odds? (p. 112)
A. 1 out of 3
B. 2 out of 8 (1 out of 4)
C. 4 out of 8 (1 out of 2)
D. 4 out of 7
E. Because there are four jacks in a 52-card
   deck
F. 13 out of 52 (1 out of 4)
G. Answers will vary.

What Are the Chances? (p. 113)
A. four; 1:4
B. one in six; 1:6
C. two in twelve; 2:12
D. black/black   white/white   black/white
E. one in 3; 1:3
F. two in three; 2:3
G. Answers will vary.

Empirical Probability (p. 114)
A. $75/100 = 300/x \Rightarrow x = 400$
B. $602/1600 = 0.37625 \approx 0.38$
C. $1600 - 128/1600 = 1472/1600 = 0.92$

Equally-Likely (p. 115)
A. $26/52 = 1/2$ B. $13/52 = 1/4$
C. $39/52 = 3/4$ D. $4/52 = 1/13$
E. $12/52 = 3/13$ F. $48/52 = 12/13$
G. $2/52 = 1/26$
H. $12 + 15 + 21 + 9 + 3 = 60$
I. $3/60 = 1/20$ J. $45/60 = 3/4$
K. $21 + 9 = 30/60 = 1/2$ L. $12/60 = 1/5$
M. $51/60 = 17/20$ N. $18/60 = 3/10$